Author biography

Manoj Kamber's Journey is an Inspiring Story of a Highly respected Entrepreneur and Founder And CEO hailing from Mumbai, Maharashtra, India. With a diverse educational background and an insatiable thirst for knowledge, he obtained a Master's degree in Computer Science from Parul University and a Master's degree in Business Administration from the European Open University. He further expanded his expertise through specialized studies in Internet of Things from Stanford University, as well as specializations in Machine Learning, Data Science, and Business and Finance from esteemed institutions such as Stanford University, Johns Hopkins University, and the Indian School of Business. Driven by his passion for Technology and Innovation, Manoj embarked on a remarkable professional journey. He served as a Google Cloud Engineer at Google India, where he contributed his expertise to cutting-edge cloud computing projects. Furthermore, he worked as a research engineer at Meta (formerly known as Facebook) in the United States, where he played a vital role in advancing research initiatives in the field of technology.

Manoj's exceptional knowledge and contributions have had a significant impact on the academic community as well. His name is referenced in an impressive 4.7 million research papers and books by academia, attesting to the depth of his expertise and the influence of his work. His innovative ideas and insights have shaped the discourse within various fields and have become a valuable resource for researchers and scholars worldwide. Currently, Manoj is the Founder & CEO of 8 Time Coding, an exceptional coding learning platform that focuses on creating reliable products for individuals embarking on their coding learning journey, seamlessly integrated with the metaverse. Additionally, he holds the prestigious position of Founder & CEO at PI-ML Research Company.

Language Nexus Unleashing Linguistic Linked Open Data

"Connecting Language and Knowledge through Collaborative Data-Intensive Research"

Manoj Kamber

ISBN 978-93-5667-936-8
© Manoj Kamber 2023

Published in India 2023 by Pencil

A brand of
One Point Six Technologies Pvt. Ltd.
Unit no. 26, Ground Floor, Building A1,
Wadala Truck Terminal Road,
Near Post Office, Antop Hill, Mumbai - 400037
E connect@thepencilapp.com
W www.thepencilapp.com

DISCLAIMER: *The opinions expressed in this book are those of the authors and do not purport to reflect the views of the Publisher.*

CONTENTS

1. Open DataLinked DataLinked Open DataLinguistic Linked Open Data (LLOD) A General Introduction

In late many years, mainstream researchers has become progressively mindful of the significance of transparency — for programming (open source), distributions (open access), organized information (open information), and information assortments overall (Open Information). Here, we center around the last angle. For sure, distributing information assortments under open assets has become daily schedule in cutting edge research. In this underlying part, we expound on inspirations and shows for distributing Open Information in etymology and related regions. The Open Information development in phonetics — as well as in every aspect of concentrate in science, calculation, and humanities — draws on three primary inspirations: (1) obligation, (2) reproducibility, and (3) reusability.

The logical interaction — the age of novel experiences, the foundation and correction of standards of thought and logical strategies, and their documentation, spread, and basic reflection — is driven by cultural, monetary, and biological need to comprehend and to foster our past, present, and future. In this sense, logical exploration accompanies both an honor and an obligation: Any ventures are upheld by open subsidizing, and consequently their outcomes ought to (and as a matter of fact are frequently expected to) become accessible to the general population. Over the most recent couple of many years, this has added to the ascent of open access in logical distributions, and, alongside it, to open source permitting of logical code and information.

One more inspiration for the rising significance of Open Information in research is inborn to the logical strategy: Logical speculations should be testable, logical hypotheses ought to be obvious, and distributed results ought to be replicable. For information driven trains, for example, exact parts of etymology, confirmation assumes the accessibility of observational information, while replicability expects admittance to the first information that the examination expands on. Albeit different dispersion and distribution models are reasonable for this reason — and have as a matter of fact been executed by organizations like the Semantic Information Consortium (LDC) or the European Language Exploration Affiliation (ELRA); by local area entryways like Perseus,1 the Cuneiform Computerized Library Initiative,2 furthermore, The Language Archive;3 or on the other hand inside appropriated local area endeavors like the All inclusive Dependencies,4 and UniMorph5 — distribution under an open source permit places the most minimal conceivable hindrance for reusability, availability, and spread of exploration information. 3. A third reasonable inspiration for distributing (and utilizing) logical information is the gigantic exertion put into making such assets and the expected increases of sharing and reusing existing information.

In a few areas of phonetics, this relates to essential information, like accounts, records, and composed message; as an outrageous model, information assortments for dialects at the edge of elimination and additionally spoken in far off region of the world are indispensable. No matter what the underlying inspiration, reusability (whether for replication studies, new applications, or novel examinations) is a definitive objective of distributing Open Information. Yet, auxiliary reuse of information isn't just a worry inside phonetics research. It is likewise an issue pertinent to any logical discipline.

As a matter of fact, how much an area of examination creates and follows settled upon standards and principles for the administration of information, as for its objective of cultivating reproducibility, can be viewed as a mark of its development as a logical discipline. For phonetics, progress toward this path includes difficulties at various levels, going from political, moral, and legitimate issues — for instance, local area shows for dealing with public and global copyright, and security issues (for exploratory information or field accounts) — to local area wide principles of best practice for documentation, support, and circulation; and past those, to the specialized inquiry of how to address, access, and incorporate existing information assortments. As an innovation, Connected Information permits us to incorporate heterogeneous information assortments facilitated by various information suppliers, and consequently normally supplements the call to Open Information in both science and society.

Connected Open Information (LOD) portrays their conjoint application to a dataset. In application to phonetically significant datasets, Etymological Connected Open Information (LLOD) depicts shows and a local area that has arisen beginning around 2010 whose most unmistakable result is the Etymological Connected Open Information cloud graph. In this volume, we portray the use of Connected (Open) Information to semantic information, specifically from the point of language procurement. Open Information in Science The Open Information development addresses a worldwide difference at the top of the priority list for how we might interpret economy, society, and science.

In the twenty-first 100 years, an original worldview that works with both straightforwardness and receptiveness has been arising. In legislative issues, this has been showed, for instance, in an expanded number of Opportunity of Data Acts or in the utilization of Right to Data Regulations, among almost 70 nations in 2006 (Banisar 2006) and in excess of 100 nations in 2018 (Banisar 2018). Similarly, the logical communis opinio is progressively moving from shut (private) information to Open Information. For its fruitful execution, open science does, notwithstanding, require local area principles on the best way to perform, archive, permit, and access information distributions.

To further develop straightforwardness and reproducibility of logical examination, a gathering of specialists teaming up with M. D. Wilkinson figured out the FAIR Core values in 2016 (Wilkinson et al. 2016). F Findability infers (1) that information and metadata are appointed universally special and interminably persevering identifiers, (2) that the information are joined by rich metadata, and that (3) the information are enlisted or filed in a site where they can be found. An Openness suggests (1) that information are retrievable by their identifier utilizing an (2) open, free, and generally executed convention, and (3) that the convention upholds validation and approval if important. I Interoperability suggests that the information are depicted utilizing a formal, open, shared, furthermore, comprehensively material language for information portrayal.

R Reusability infers expansion of precise and applicable properties, clear authorizing and information use agreements, a connecting to provenance of information, and adherence to local area guidelines. Connected Information addresses a specialized structure that permits clients to handle these difficulties both overall and for the particular necessities of semantics and language innovation. Connected Information Quite a bit of the present information are accessible in dissipated vaults and in different organizations. numerous possibly important datasets are being made or partaken in information designs expected for human utilization instead of for robotized handling.

For instance, electronic version by means of PDF (Compact Record Configuration) is as yet thought about cutting edge in different disciplines in the humanities; and routinely, accounting sheet or office programming is utilized to make what's more, to fill structures and tables of those PDF records, with no conventional information structures. Similarly, a well known piece of programming in semantics is upgraded for human utilization as opposed to for machine meaningfulness: The Field Etymologist's Toolbox6 gives wordand morpheme-level sparkling functionalities. Its fundamental organization, be that as it may, is a plain text design, and the arrangement between various layers of morpheme comment is finished through whitespaces. Be that as it may, its ongoing text style affects the width of the text shown, and whitespace arrangement between, say, morpheme division and morpheme sparkling, or between morpheme division and word division, must be reproduced if the specific widths of each person and each whitespace in the fundamental textual style are known.

Sadly, numerous text styles utilize variable person width, so that, as a rule, Tool compartment division can't be dependably deciphered or changed over into different

configurations. These hardships compare to issues and needs connected with the Trap of Archives overall. In the first place, it isn't machine-lucid in light of the fact that the information are unstructured. Second, the information are separated. Just archives are connected and the implications of the connections are not satisfactory. Third, just a text search is at present plausible. A proposed answer for these issues is to supplement the Snare of Reports with the Snare of Information, directed by Connected Information standards. The expression "Connected Information" was initially distributed in 2006 as a Plan Issue by Tim Berners-Lee (2006) and gives a set of four standards of best practice to be adhered to for the distribution of information on the web. In a somewhat reformulated structure, these guidelines are recreated underneath.

Uniform Asset Identifiers: Use URIs for recognizing information and relations. 2. Resolvable by means of

HTTP(S): Use HTTP(S) URIs so that individuals can look into those names. 3. Normalized designs: For any URI in a dataset, give valuable data utilizing RDF-based principles. 4. Joins: Incorporate connections to other URIs, with the goal that clients can find more things. A Uniform Asset Identifier (URI; Berners-Lee et al. 2005) is a smaller grouping of characters that distinguishes a theoretical or actual asset. An outright URI starts with a convention or a plan name (e.g., https) trailed by a power (e.g., en.wikipedia.org) what's more, a way (e.g.,/wiki/Linguistic_Linked_Open_Data), trailed by a discretionary question (headed by ?) and a section (headed by #, e.g., #Linguistic_Linked_Open _Data): https://en.wikipedia.org/wiki/Semantic _ Connected _ Open _ Information #Semantic _ Connected _ Open _ Information This model outlines that the ordinary type of a URI in a Connected Information setting is a Uniform Asset Finder (URL; Berners-Lee et al. 1994).

URLs characterize a subset of URIs that recognize an asset, yet in addition give a method for finding it by portraying its essential access system (for this situation, the HTTPS convention). The URI standard is supplemented by Internationalized Asset Identifiers (IRIs; Duerst and Suignard 2005), which broaden the extent of reasonable characters to Unicode: Non-ASCII characters are planned to ASCII get away from successions through the URI percent encoding, concerning model the image $\bar{g}$ (Unicode character U+1E21, UTF-8 E1B8A1) as %E1%B8%A1. The third rule endorses the utilization of specific norms. In its unique plan, the guidelines RDF (information model) and SPARQL (inquiry language) were named. Consequently, be that as it may, extra norms have been created.

Subsequently, we decipher this standard these days such that each datum design for which a W3C-normalized understanding as RDF information exists ought to be a feasible choice. This incorporates local RDF serializations, for example, Turtle,7 JSON-LD,8 or then again RD F/XML;9 dialects that grant the installing of RDF content;10 planning dialects to deliver RDF information from other formats;11 dialects that are characterized based on RDF;12 and RDF-based question languages.13 As information from different sources (CSV documents, XML, social data sets, RDF-local information) can be flawlessly con-verted between various RDF serializations, RDF-based portrayal formalisms empower information, data customers, and processors the same to get to, decipher, and change data in an adaptable, serialization-free way.

The RDF information model formalizes named coordinated multi-diagrams, or at least, hubs (RDF assets) and relations (RDF properties) that hold between them. The two hubs and relations are recognized through URIs, and a triple of source hub ("subject"), connection ("property") and target hub ("object") is an assertion: . #

marks end of proclamation, remarks later # This model is written in Turtle documentation, with whitespace-isolated full URIs and . to mark the finish of the assertion. Furthermore, Turtle gives various reasonable shorthands, for instance the presentation of prefixes. The accompanying Turtle section is subsequently same:

PREFIX wpedia: PREFIX foaf: PREFIX dbpedia: wpedia:Linguistic _ Connected _ Open _ Information foaf:primaryTopic dbpedia:Linguistic _ Connected _ Open _ Information . RDF triples can likewise take another structure, where a source hub ("subject") is doled out a exacting worth instead of an objective hub: PREFIX rdfs: wpedia:Linguistic _ Connected _ Open _ Information rdfs:label "Semantic Connected Open Data"@en. A few assertions can likewise be conjoined through a semicolon ; (same subject, different property, different item) or a comma (same subject, same property, different item): wpedia:Linguistic _ Connected _ Open _ Information foaf:primaryTopic dbpedia:Linguistic _ Connected _ Open _ Information ; rdfs:label "Semantic Connected Open Data"@en. The fourth rule requires some genuine connecting, that is to say, the production of cross-references between various, dispersed datasets, hence empowering a Snare of Information to emerge along and close to the Trap of Archives. This is represented in the model above, where a Wikipedia URL and a DBpedia URI are being associated with the RDF property foaf:primaryTopic. The vital distinction between RDF connections and HTML hyperlinks is that the previous are semantically composed. Subsequently, a machine-comprehensible, semantically characterized chart portrayal is made for them, which isn't just valuable for asset coordination on the Trap of Information, yet additionally an exceptionally conventional information structure that tracks down prompt application in semantics.

In reality the connecting system gives fascinating potential outcomes to logical datasets, including allowing quick admittance to remote datasets and phrasing bases. In along these lines, it becomes conceivable to share identifiers and to recognize ideas and elements relating with one another, and in this manner to orchestrate dispersed datasets not just on the level of organization and method for access, yet additionally on a reasonable level, through the utilization of (or then again reference to) existing vocabularies. Area wording gave in a metaphysics, for model, can be connected to nonexclusive information bases like the DBpedia,14 and in this manner advanced with DBpedia data. For example, expect that we have both a meaning of "(mechanical) peculiarity" in an English thesaurus and its connecting with the English DBpedia: PREFIX owl: PREFIX my: my:singularity owl:sameAs dbpedia:Technological _ peculiarity.

As the English DBpedia gives a German mark, we can promptly return the German names to our thesaurus ideas and hence apply them to the examination of another dialect. This is carried out in the accompanying SPARQL question: PREFIX owl: PREFIX rdfs: SELECT ?mySingularity ?germanLabel WHERE { # for all owl:sameAs joins ?mySingularity owl:sameAs ?dbpediaResource. # find the rdfs names of the articles ?dbpediaResource rdfs:label ?germanLabel. FILTER(lang(?germanLabel,'de')) # what's more, limit the outcome to German language } In like manner, enormous size data sets — of, say, qualities, proteins, geological names, or even film titles — can be connected over various dialects and coordinated with one another, so that data from different sources supplements one another.

There are a few reasons for distributing Connected Information: First, it permits simplicity of revelation through connecting. Second, it is not difficult to consume by the two people and machines. Third, it lessens excess exploration also, upholds coordinated effort. Fourth, it adds worth, perceivability, and effect. Obviously, Connected Information isn't obliged to Open Information, be that as it may, clearly, distributing information under open licenses works with their availability for ensuing variation and improvement. However, it is critical to recall that not all Connected Information are open and that authorized information can in any case benefit from utilizing guidelines (enhanced with connections to Connected Information or potentially gotten to by standard tools).

Linked Open Information The meaning of Connected Open Information (LOD) is Connected Information that are transparently authorized. In 2010, Tim Berners-Lee (Berners-Lee 2006) expanded his unique Connected Information portrayal with a subsequent part on Open Information. Connected Open Information (LOD) is Connected Information that are delivered under an open permit, for example, characterized by the Open Definition,15 where "open means anybody can uninhibitedly access, use, change, and offer for any reason (subject, probably, to prerequisites that save provenance and transparency)."

For limited time reasons, the level of LOD consistence is communicated by a star plot, by which an information distributer gets 1 to 5 stars (*), as indicated by the accompanying necessities: * information accessible as

Open Information on the web (e.g., as an output) ** if * utilizing machine-meaningful, organized design (e.g., DOCX) *** on the off chance that ** utilizing non-exclusive arrangement (e.g., HTML) **** in the event that *** utilizing open, RDF-based principles ***** if **** in addition to connecting with others' information Furthermore, information distributers are urged to distribute information alongside their metadata also, to enroll these metadata in significant inventories like

http://datahub.io/ , or, for etymological information, in http://linghub.org. From these archives, the LOD (resp., LLOD) graphs are being created. Connected Open Information has turned into a pattern in logical exploration and foundations during the 2010s, with noticeable assets like DBpedia (Lehmann et al. 2009), created inside an open-source project with the very name that focused on separated organized information from Wikipedia and related assets. DBpedia form 2016-10 remembers extractions for 134 dialects with a sum of north of 13 billion RDF proclamations (significantly increases). With to an ever increasing extent datasets being connected with DBpedia and other LOD datasets, a Connected Open Information cloud has arisen, and as a perception of the developing Trap of Open Information, this cycle has been reported with a progression of LOD cloud diagrams.

16 As of October 2018, the graph contained 1,229 datasets with 16,125 connections (figure 1.1). Essential utilizations of RDF innovation and LOD assets are worried

about asset combination and furthermore with asset reuse. Thus, significant parts of the LOD cloud chart are term bases like measurable government information, or biomedical data sets, and without a doubt the vital benefit of RDF innovation and LOD assets is their elevated degree of reusability and openness. SPARQL 1.1 upholds the idea of organization: Through the Help catchphrase, it is feasible to counsel outside SPARQL endpoints (RDF information bases with web interfaces) as a feature of a inquiry against a nearby triple (or quad) store. Truth be told, assets can be uninhibitedly shared and cloned, and excess duplicates can contribute to the manageability of LOD datasets freely from the foundation that initially given those information or their specialized frameworks.

Without a doubt, such excess duplicates are ordinarily made as LOD are handled: While the SPARQL 1.1 convention permits clients to get to far off SPARQL

endpoints through the Administration watchword, and far off RDF dumps through Burden, both accompany a specific level of above, and in this way lead to runtime decreases for applications that consume Connected Information. Genuine uses of LOD along these lines regularly work on nearby duplicates, all things being equal, so repetitive and circulated duplicates are made as a result of LOD-based applications. For logical applications, one more element of LOD is significant — that will be, that unique applications can allude to a similar term in a similar data set. Hence results, information, and comments can be in every way followed over various datasets while data about them can be put in connection with one another.

Obviously, a similar applies, even to a bigger degree, to vocabularies utilized for various assets. With expanded reusability and reuse of logical datasets, the datasets act as models for the jargon of ensuing assets, and to be sure research in local area based jargon advancement has escalated as of late. We likewise should concede that LOD accompanies various specialized difficulties. LOD and RDF innovation both give a significant level view as well as a conventional innovation for handling and incorporating various information sources, and obviously "genericity" accompanies a cost. The capability of RDF and RDF-based innovation in contrast with old style social data sets can in this way measure up to the additions and difficulties of significant level programming dialects (like Java or Python) in contrast with low-level programming dialects, (for example, machine code or constructing agent).

In any case, for some issues, handling RDF (cf. Python) will be significantly more slow than utilizing an execution explicit SQL cular (cf. constructing agent), however it succeeds in versatility, reusability, and improvement exertion. Specifically, RDF is predominant at managing inadequate and heterogeneous information, yet for thickly populated data sets, RDF innovation is delayed in correlation with old style social data set innovation. Not at all like SQL, RDF innovation permits clients verna to connect past an information storehouse and to consistently connect information with outside assets. One explicit test in this setting is that connections among assets and assets themselves were made for various purposes, as indicated by various approaches and are kept up with by various suppliers.

This can prompt irregularities in the understanding and in the nature of proclamations (significantly increases) they give. An inexorably significant viewpoint is consequently the following of provenance and related metadata, so that logical and industry applications the same can (and ought to) assess the arrangement of information collected from LOD and should not indiscriminately depend on their rightness. In rundown, Connected Open Information is empowering a difference in information and data perusers what's more, processors in that it empowers us to extract from asset explicit arrangements and portrayals and advances, and afterward to coordinate data over dispersed datasets. Connected Open Information addresses the center of the arising Web of Information and in this manner empowers a worldwide difference in information and data the board and handling.

LOD accompanies rich mechanical help, regarding versatile method for access and portrayal (W3Cstandardized information models, configurations, conventions, and question dialects), concerning specialized support with off-the-rack data sets, and as far as the presence of an extensive designer and client local area. Simultaneously, numerous logical moves corresponding to LOD center strategies appear to have been settled, so the concentration in LOD research has moved from establishments and fundamental norms to applications. A new improvement in this respect is the distribution of space explicit sub-mists, which since August 2018 have been accessible as LOD addenda graphs.

Phonetic Connected Open Information addresses one such area of utilization. Connected Open Information in Phonetics As is valid for any field of logical examination, the FAIR standards are applicable for semantics, language studies, and regular language handling — that is, for the advanced language assets they produce and expand on — and for sure Bird and Simons (2003) figured out equivalent prerequisites and best practice proposals for language assets a long time back, which we have revamped and marginally rephrased beneath as per the FAIR standards. All things considered, RDF and (Phonetic) Connected (Open) Information give an optimal structure to execute these prerequisites. In the list beneath, this is shown with a $\pm$ positioning going from $-$to $+++$. 17 F findability presence at an information provider++ :

Register language assets at a significant asset gateway. In a Semantic Connected Open Information setting, this would be LingHub (http://linghub.org/) or on the other hand one of the asset gateways it constructs on.18 pertinence/discovery+ : Give metadata as per local area endorsed shows and vocabularies. persistence+ : Give tenacious identifiers to language assets (e.g., a constant URL) and extraordinary identifiers for parts of a language asset. long haul preservation+ : Give long haul protection by facilitating at an establishment focused on that reason. An openness open format+++ : Give information in an open arrangement upheld by numerous apparatuses. complete access+ :

Give direct admittance to the full information and documentation. unobstructed access+++ : Give documentation about the strategies for access. widespread access+++ : Give all inclusive admittance to each intrigued client. I interoperability terminology++ : Guide phonetic terms and markup components to a typical cosmology. design documentation+++ : Give information in a self-depicting design (counting XML, RDF, JSON). machine-meaningful format+++ : Utilize open norms, for example, those given by the W3C (Unicode, XML, and so forth.). comprehensible format+ : Give intelligible renditions of the material. R reusability rich content++ :19 Give rich and etymologically important substance. accountability+ : Completely report both the asset and its source information. provenance+ : Give provenance and attribution metadata. immutability+ : Give permanent, fixed forms of an asset, with suitable forming. lawful documentation+++ :

Report protected innovation privileges of all parts of the language asset. research license+++ : Guarantee that the asset might be utilized for research purposes. complete preservation+++ : Ensure that all parts of the language asset and its documentation stay open from now on (i.e., autonomous from a specific programming). Current availability challenges emerge in the various configurations and plans of reports, their conveyance, and the scattered idea of metadata assortments. There have long been endeavors to perceive and resolve these issues, yet these exercises were never facilitated. Specifically, RDF was utilized, however assets were seldom connected to other assets in the Trap of Information. So a local area should have been constructed. Starting around 2010, the rising prominence of applying RDF to language assets and the potential for making joins between various datasets drove

(1) to the development of the Open Phonetics Working Gathering of Open Information International20 and, in this way

(2) to the rise of a Semantic Connected Open Information (LLOD) cloud, as well as

(3) to the advancement of local area shows for the distribution of etymologically applicable datasets on the Snare of Information. Open Information Worldwide is a charitable association, established in 2004, that advances open information in the entirety of its structures (e.g., distribution of government information in the UK and USA); it gives infrastructural backing to a few working gatherings. The Open Phonetics Working Gathering of the Open Information Establishment (OWLG) was coordinated in October 2010 in Berlin, Germany, and collected an organization of people keen on semantic assets and additionally their distribution under open licenses. The OWLG is multidisciplinary and has foundation in the types of a mailing list and a website.21 Its most significant exercises are the association of local area occasions like studios, datathons/summer schools what's more, gatherings, and the continuous advancement of the Phonetic Connected Open Information (sub-) cloud, at present kept up with under http://etymological lod.org/. The Etymological Connected Open Information (LLOD, figure 1.2) cloud is an assortment of semantic assets that have been distributed under open licenses as Connected Information.

It is decentralized in its turn of events and support and was created as a local area exertion with regards to the Open

Etymology Working Gathering of the Open Information Establishment. At first, the OWLG kept a rundown of open or delegate assets; in January 2011, this gathering stamped potential collaborations between these assets in the principal draft of a LLOD cloud graph. As of now, it was only a dream, and the draft included non-open assets as placeholders for different assets to come, however none have been understood. In the end section of their contributed volume on Connected Information in Etymology, Chiarcos, Nordhoff, and Hellmann (2012) gave a speculative connecting to chose datasets from NLP, Semantic Web, and etymological typology portrayed in the book.

In September 2012, theLLOD cloud chart emerged because of the first datathon on Multilingual Connected Open Information for Endeavors (MLODE-2012). Beginning around 2012, more information and more inflexible quality imperatives have been added, joint efforts with public and global examination projects have been laid out, and related W3C local gatherings have arisen. With the rising notoriety of LLOD, in August 2014 "phonetics" was perceived as a high level classification of the shaded LOD cloud graph, with LLOD assets previously having been grouped into different classes. In August 2018, a duplicate of the LLOD cloud chart was integrated into the LOD cloud graph as a space explicit addendum. Inside the LOD cloud, Semantic Connected Open Information is developing at a somewhat high rate. While the yearly development of the LOD cloud (as far as new assets added) over the last two years has been at 10.2% on normal for the LOD cloud graph, the LLOD cloud graph itself has been developing at 19.3% each year (cf. figure 1.3).

Beside its keeping up with the LLOD cloud chart, the OWLG plans to advance open phonetic assets by bringing issues to light and gathering metadata, and means to work with a extensive variety of local area exercises by facilitating studios, utilizing its broad mailing list, making different distributions. In doing as such, they work with trade between and among more particular local gatherings, for example, the W3C local gatherings (for example, the Cosmology Lexica Local gathering (OntoLex),22 the Connected Information for Innovation Working Bunch [LD4LT],23 or the Accepted procedures for Multilingual Connected Open Information People group Bunch [BPM-LOD]).24 At the hour of composing, the most dynamic of these W3C local gatherings is the OntoLex bunch, which is creating determinations for lexical information in a LOD setting; this need connects with the high fame among LLOD assets of the OntoLex jargon (Cimiano, McCrae, and Buitelaar 2016).

While details for lexical assets are somewhat full grown, as are term bases for either language assortments (de Melo 2015; Nordhoff what's more, Hammarström 2011) or etymological phrasing (Aguado de Cea, Álvarez de Mon, Gómez-Pérez, and Pareja-Lora 2004; Chiarcos 2008; Chiarcos and Sukhareva 2015), the interaction of growing generally applied information models for different sorts of language assets, like corpora and information assortments by and large, is as yet continuous. Partially, this volume means to add to this conversation and its future turn of events. Possibilities, Difficulties, and Possibilities The singular commitments thus archive progress made in the field of Phonetic Connected Open Information starting around 2012 (Chiarcos et al. 2012). One significant contrast in contrast with improvements in that year — when the local area was generally fabricating on limited scope tests and envisioning a splendid vision representing things to come — is that suppliers of existing frameworks and of existing stages are progressively engaging in both the cycle and the conversation; this is reflected by the supporters of this volume. The overall circumstance is that a noteworthy measure of Etymological Connected Open Information is currently accessible, a sum that proceeds to develop consistently. In a more drawn out viewpoint, we can anticipate that extra information suppliers should offer a L(O)D view on their information, and to help RDF serializations, for example, JSON-LD as trade designs. Nonetheless, LOD's further development and prevalence rely urgently upon the improvement of utilizations that are prepared to do either consuming these information in an etymologist well disposed style or of enhancing nearby information with far reaching web assets.

At the hour of composing, working with RDF ordinarily requires a specific degree of specialized mastery — at least, essential information on SPARQL and of somewhere around one RDF design. The creators' very own involvement with showing college courses demonstrates the way that etymologists can be effectively prepared to get both. In any case, this isn't regularly finished and is probably not going to at any point be a piece of the phonetics central subjects. This might change once assigned course books on Connected Open Information for NLP and for semantics become accessible, however for the time being vital for this work and the more extensive local area stays to give substantial applications custom fitted to the requirements of language specialists, etymologists, scientists in NLP, and information engineers. Promising methodologies toward this path do exist: Existing devices can be supplemented with a RDF layer to work with their interoperability. This is the extent of a few sections in this volume. Similarly, LLOD-local applications are conceivable — for example, to utilize RDFa (RDF in credits; Herman et al. 2015) to supplement a XML work process with SPARQL-based semantic inquiry through web administrations (Tittel et al. 2018); to give total, enhancement, and quest schedules for language asset metadata (Chiarcos et al.

2016; McCrae and Cimiano 2015); to involve RDF as a formalism for comment incorporation and information the board (Burchardt et al. 2008; Pareja-Lora 2012; Chiarcos et al. 2017); or on the other hand to utilize RDF and SPARQL for controlling and assessing semantic comments (Chiarcos, Khait et al. 2018; Chiarcos, Kosmehl et al. 2018). While these applications exhibit the capability of LOD innovation in etymology, they accompany an extensive section hindrance, and they address the high level client of RDF innovation as opposed to an ordinary language specialist. Despite the fact that substantial applications do exist, the way stays long to coming to the level of ease of use that infrequent clients of this innovation could anticipate.

A prominent exemption in such manner is LexO (Bellandi, Giovannetti, and Piccini 2018), a graphical device for cooperatively altering lexical and ontological assets that locally expand on the OntoLex jargon and RDF; LexO was intended to direct lexicographical work in a philological setting (for example, making the Dictionnaire des Termes Médico-botaniques de l'Ancien Occitan). Different activities whose goal is to give LLOD-based devices for explicit areas of use have been as of late supported, so progress toward this path is cheerfully not out of the ordinary inside the following years.25 Affirmations

This section begins from a joint show given by Antonio Pareja-Lora, Martin Brümmer, and Christian Chiarcos at the 2015 LSA studio named "Improvement of Phonetic Connected Open Information (LLOD) Assets for Cooperative Information Escalated Exploration in the Language Sciences." From one viewpoint, crafted by the main creator has been somewhat upheld by the German Government Service for Science and Schooling (BMBF) in the setting of the Exploration Gathering Connected Open Word references (LiODi, 2015-2020). On the other hand, crafted by the subsequent creator has been to some extent upheld by the ventures RedR+Human (Progressively Reconfigurable Instructive Stores in the Humanities, ref. TIN2014-52010-R) and CetrO+Spec (Creation, Investigation and Change of Instructive Article Stores in Specific Spaces, ref. TIN2017-88092-R), both supported by the Spanish Service of Economy and Intensity.

2. Whither GOLD

Be that as it may, my two recently enrolled research colleagues, Scott Farrar and Will Lewis, rapidly persuaded me that a superior way is exploit the framework of the Semantic Web declared in Berners-Lee, Hendler, and Lassila (2001) that was a work in progress as a thinking stage for all freely shared information on the web. In particular, we would start to fabricate a philosophy for the ideas required for semantic investigation as a subcomponent of an upper philosophy, for example, of SUMO, the Standard Upper Consolidated Philosophy (Pease and Niles 2002; Pease 2007).

This philosophy, similar to SUMO and like other space explicit web ontologies, would be written in one of the markup dialects being built for the Semantic Web, like OWL-DL, not in XML. In fact, this did not disregard the E-Merge task's underwriting of XML as the markup language of decision for semantic comment. Such comment might in any case be written in XML however the translation of its labels not set in stone by the ideas they alluded to (i.e., highlighted) in GOLD. FS would be treated as an information type, with not entirely set in stone by its associations with GOLD. In Lewis, Langendoen, and Farrar (2001), our most memorable show following the opening shot gathering, we brought up that the genuine need of the local area we were serving would be "to acquire data about imperiled dialects on the Around the world Web regardless of the labeling plans that are utilized in the different sites they counsel. Subsequently [we] can't force a markup standard for imperiled language sites, indeed, even verifiably by fostering an information exchange design [such as the TEI]."

To seem OK of this markup tumult, we proposed the improvement of a "metatagging" plot comprising of "an information base and its going with devices [that] will go about as an interlingua for information correlation," the way to which is a philosophy. At the time we presented the paper for show, we had previously made a philosophy for morphosyntactic ideas with many hubs drawn from assets given by the Mid year Organization of Semantics and the Dokumentation Bedrohter Sprachen (DOBES) project, two general etymology term sets and a few word references and syntaxes of jeopardized dialects, yet we had not yet given it a name. At the studio, we declared our decision: the Overall Cosmology for Semantic Portrayal (GOLD). The Advancement of GOLD inside the E-Merge Undertaking Introductions about GOLD were made at each yearly E-Merge studio from 2002 through the finish of the venture in 2006, as well as at various meetings and studios all over the planet, including Langendoen, Farrar, and Lewis (2002), Farrar, Lewis, and Langendoen (2002), Farrar and Langendoen (2004), Simons et al.

(2004b), and Lewis (2006). GOLD came to the consideration of the phonetics local area on the loose through the distribution of Farrar and Langendoen (2003), and the Etymologist Rundown started facilitating GOLD's site in 2006.6 Two significant achievements happened during this period. Initial, a proof of idea was accomplished for the metatagging plan proposed in Lewis, Langendoen, what's more, Farrar (2001) to do look over contrastingly encoded datasets of IGT and electronic word references (Simons et al. 2004a, 2004b). Second, the Web-based Data set of Interlinear Text (ODIN) was set up, in which clients could choose from a rundown of

GOLD morphosyntactic ideas and find examples of IGT gathered from the web in excess of 700 dialects that contain morphemes referring to them (Lewis 2006). Nonetheless, minimal other advancement was made past the further refinements of the reasonable design for morphosyntax, a circumstance that has proceeded right up to the present day.

GOLD after E-Merge At the finish of the E-Merge project in 2006, Scott Farrar proceeded with his work for a few additional years on GOLD's calculated spine, especially on the idea of the phonetic sign itself (Farrar 2007), and on the overall benefits of the different forms of OWL for executing GOLD (Farrar and Langendoen 2010). Will Lewis alongside Fei Xia and different associates have stretched out the ODIN's information inclusion to almost 1,300 dialects and more than 130,000 examples (Lewis and Xia 2010; Xia et al. 2014).

7 At last, the Lexical Improvement through the GOLD Philosophy (LEGO) project — started in 2008 under the course of two of the E-Merge head agents, Anthony Aristar and Helen AristarDry, along with Jeff Great — has labeled the passages of 12 vocabularies and 11 wordlists

with connections to GOLD ideas to help cross-etymological pursuit much in the way of ODIN.8 Neither task, in any case, has broadened GOLD's applied inclusion. What's Straightaway? The subject of how to support the GOLD exertion toward the finish of the E-Merge project was considered by Farrar and Lewis (2007), who recommended that networks of training get a sense of ownership with developing GOLD subcomponents for specific dialects and language families, and team up on figuring out which cross-semantic develops ought to be integrated into GOLD itself.

In any case, no compelling move has yet been made on their suggestions. Drinking spree and Langendoen (2010: sec. 4) imagined a future examination climate for etymologists called Computerized Framework that upholds Phonetic Request (DILI) that forms on past and current work and gives the accompanying three limits, among others: 1. Prepared admittance to a lot of computerized information in text, sound, and sound video media about numerous dialects, which are pertinent to a wide range of areas of examination and application both inside and beyond semantics. 2. Offices for looking at, consolidating, and dissecting information across media, dialectts, and subdisciplines, and endeavors to improve DILI with their outcomes. 3. Administrations to help consistent joint effort across space, time, (sub)disciplines, and hypothetical points of view. We proceeded to say, "It isn't needed that there be a solitary overall organization for all the explanations in DILI, however it would be alluring if sense would be made of the relations among calculated networks for various explanation plans, especially those that address different hypothetical viewpoints.... This perspective on the job of applied encoding was as of late expressed in Farrar and Lewis (200[7]), alongside an arrangement for how to accomplish it."

In case this vision be excused as fantasy dream, we called attention to that correspondingly aggressive exploration conditions as of now exist for such fields as organic chemistry, nanotechnology, and space science — so why not etymology? Maybe the absence of such examination conditions in phonetics is a consequence of the long history of our field, which jumped up freely in shifting language and social networks in a few regions of the planet, or maybe it's the touchiness of us etymologists, or indeed, even the thought that it's harder for our own than for the overwhelming majority of others' fields of request. I consider Scott Farrar, battling with the issue of describing the thought of the etymological sign for use in GOLD, who at long last formed something that came genuinely close to what Louis Hjelmslev (1943 [1962]) proposed. Assuming that Farrar is to some degree in the right ballpark, then, at that point, the hidden rationale should be more extravagant than that given by OWL-DL, which is a decidable variant of first-request rationale, in any event, setting to the side the wondrous intricacies of the coherent structures expected to address, for instance, equal developments on the planet's languages.

9 The explanation is that Farrar's structures need to connect with one another compositionally, both for significance and for expression.

10 The sythesis of implications is represented by whatever reasonable (sensible) activity is called for to join them, like restricting a predicate variable by a quantifier.

Simultaneously, the arrangement of articulations is administered by a mereological (likewise coherent, yet with an alternate fractional requesting) activity, for example, link, on the off chance that the articulations are addressed as strings, so that no less than two unmistakable coherent frameworks must be synchronized. The test, I think, is definitely worth endeavor, beginning with our investigating the legitimate method for building reasonable organizations for etymological examination and comment. Notes 1. E-Merge was financed by the US Public Science Establishment award 0094934 to Wayne State College with a subcontract to the College of Arizona.

TEI was supported by the US Public Blessing for the Humanities, Directorate General XIII of the Commission of the European People group, Andrew W. Mellon Establishment, and Sociology and Humanities Exploration Gathering of Canada. 3. As seat of the TEI Council on Text Examination and Translation and of the Work Gathering on Etymological Depiction, I had generally speaking liability regarding the arrangement of these parts. The editors furthermore, the individuals from the board of trustees and of the work bunch were dynamic donors, especially Mitch Marcus, who convincingly contended for the significance of FS at the main work bunch meeting, furthermore, Gary Simons, who demonstrated the way that arrangements of FS can be approved by FSD, the last option being active (incomplete) syntaxes of the dialects portrayed by those FS sets; see Langendoen and Simons (1995). Mitch Marcus and I gave an instructional exercise named "Labeling Phonetic Data in a Message Corpus" at the June 1990 leg tendon gathering in Pittsburgh, where we depicted the rules in planning for both the Penn Treebank (PTB) and the TEI proposals for SAM and FS. The PTB, along

3. Management, Sustainability, and Interoperability of Linguistic Annotations

Presentation Lately, a recognizable rise has happened in etymological comment movement, which has extended to cover a wide assortment of etymological peculiarities. Simultaneously, the number and size of semantically commented on language assets has expanded decisively, along with an expansion of comment devices to help the creation and capacity of marked information, different means for cooperative and dispersed explanation endeavors, and the presentation of publicly supporting systems, like Amazon Mechanical Turk. All of this has made a need to oversee and support these assets, as well as to track down approaches to empower them to be more than once reused and converged with different assets.

What Is Linguistic Annotation?

Etymological explanation includes the relationship of spellbinding or scientific documentations with language information. The crude information might be printed, drawn from any source or type, or it could be as time capabilities (sound, video, as well as physiological accounts). The actual comments might incorporate records of assorted types (going from phonetic highlights to talk structures), grammatical form and sense labels, syntactic investigations, "named element" names, semantic job marks, time and occasion recognizable proof, co-reference chains, discourselevel examinations, and numerous others. Assets fluctuate in the scope of comment types they contain: A few assets contain only a couple of types, while others contain numerous comment "layers," or "levels," of etymological depictions. Semantic explanation of language information was initially acted to give data for the turn of events and testing of etymological hypotheses, or, as it is known today, corpus semantics. At that point, significant time and exertion was expected to clarify information with even the most straightforward semantic peculiarities, and the commented on corpora accessible for study were tiny.

Throughout recent many years, be that as it may, propels in processing power and capacity, along with improvement of strong techniques for programmed explanation, have made phonetically commented on information progressively accessible in steadily developing quantities.As an outcome, these assets presently serve etymological examinations as well as the field of regular language handling (NLP), which depends on semantically explained message and discourse corpora to assess new human language advances and, urgently, to create solid measurable models for preparing these advancements. An etymological explanation conspire is made out of two primary parts: the plan's semantics, which determine the classifications and highlights that mark and give spellbinding data about the information with which they are related, and the plan's portrayal, which is the actual organization wherein the comment data is addressed for utilization by programming (and, now and again, by people also).

All things considered, architects of phonetic explanation plans have zeroed in on deciding the proper classifications and elements to depict the peculiarity being referred to and stand out to the inevitable actual portrayal of the comment data, with perhaps accidental outcomes when limitations forced by the actual portrayal influence decisions for the reasonable substance of an explanation conspire. Lately, the need to think about and consolidate comments, as well as to involve them in programming conditions for which they might have not been initially planned, has expanded, prompting the mindfulness that a calculated plan might be addressed in any of a wide range of actual configurations as well as transduced from one to the next. Both the language structure and the semantics of a comment conspire include decisions that are, to some degree, inconsistent, yet that by and by have consequences for their ease of use. With respect to the actual configuration, the main decision is whether to embed the explanation data into the actual information or to address it in deadlock structure — that is, gave in a different report with connections to the situations in the first information to which every comment applies. History During the 20th 100 years, phonetics was rehearsed principally as an unmistakable field, concentrating on primary properties inside a language and typological varieties between dialects.

This work brought about genuinely refined models of the different instructive parts involving etymological expressions. As in the other sociologies, the assortment and examination of information were additionally exposed to quantitative strategies from measurements, what's more, during the 1940s, language specialists, for example, Leonard Bloomfield and others were beginning to think that language could be made sense of in probabilistic and behaviorist terms. Simultaneously, in the related and arising field of NLP Warren Weaver proposed utilizing PCs to decipher records between regular human dialects; in 1949 he delivered an update named "Interpretation" (Weaver 1955), which illustrated a progression of techniques for that task. Exact and measurable strategies stayed well known all through the 1950s, and Claude Shannon's data hypothetical view to language investigation gave a strong quantitative approach for demonstrating subjective depictions of language. Nonetheless, datasets were by and large so little that it was unrealistic to separate measurably huge examples to help probabilistic methodologies, and accordingly, semantically commented on corpora didn't assume a significant part in the primary long stretches of NLP (1950s-1960s). During the 1960s, there was a general change in the sociologies, especially in the US, from information situated depictions of human way of behaving to thoughtful displaying of mental capabilities.

As a feature of this new mentality toward human action, the US etymologist Noam Chomsky zeroed in on both a proper procedure and a hypothesis of phonetics that overlooked quantitative language information, yet additionally guaranteed that it was in fact deceiving for figuring out models of language conduct. Chomsky's view was persuasive in the US all through the following twenty years, to a great extent on the grounds that the conventional methodology empowered the improvement of very modern rule-based language models utilizing generally contemplative (or self-produced) information, along these lines giving an alluring option to making factual language models based on generally little datasets of etymological expressions from the current corpora in the field. In NLP, the thriving field of fake knowledge (simulated intelligence) started to tackle the issue of language understanding and, in the soul of the times, artificial intelligence advocates deserted experimental strategies and grounded their plan of language handling frameworks in proper hypotheses of human language figuring out, which thus they endeavored to demonstrate. IBM's advocating of measurable techniques for discourse handling during the 1970s and '80s was one of only a handful of exceptional endeavors that evaded this pattern during that time. Sensibly huge etymologically explained assets were somewhat intriguing; a wellknown special case is the 1,000,000 word Earthy colored Corpus of Standard American English (Kučera and Francis 1967).

During the 1970s, the Earthy colored Corpus was the object of what is apparently the main current semantic explanation project, which added grammatical feature annotations.1 Like the Earthy colored Corpus, corpora created during the 1970s and '80s were commonly explained exclusively for grammatical feature, in light of the fact that the absence of sensibly exact programmed techniques as well as the significant expense of manual explanation didn't allow the development of adequately enormous corpora containing explanations for other etymological peculiarities, for example, syntax.2 This changed in the mid-to late-1980s, when huge scope language information assets begun to open up. This prompted an expansion of etymological comment projects, the majority of them actually centered around grammatical feature (or more extravagant morphosyntactic) comments, and thus this initiated the renewed introduction of probabilistic strategies for programmed comment in light of measurable information got from the corpus. The main significant exertion of this sort created morphosyntactic and syntactic explanations of the 1,000,000 word LancasterOslo-Bergen (Heave) corpus of English (Garside 1987).

Expanding on this work, the Penn Treebank project (Marcus, Marcinkiewicz, and Santorini 1993) created a one-millionword corpus of Money Road Diary articles clarified for grammatical feature and skeletal syntactic explanations and, later, likewise explained for essential utilitarian data (Marcus et al. 1994). Naturally created comments consequently approved by people (in entire or to a limited extent) were utilized to make a few other significant corpora during the 1990s, including the 100-million-word English Public Corpus (Clear 1993), delivered in 1994; corpora delivered by the MULTEXT project (1993-96; Ide and Véronis 1994) and its follow-on, MULTEXT-EAST (1994-1997; Erjaveç and Ide 1998), which gave equal adjusted corpora in twelve Western and Eastern dialects clarified for grammatical feature; and the PAROLE and Straightforward corpora,3 which included grammatical form labeled information in fourteen European dialects. Following these endeavors, syntactic treebanks for a wide assortment of dialects (e.g., Swedish, Czech, Chinese,

French, German, Spanish, Turkish, Italian) multiplied over the course of the following ten years, along with corpora explained for different peculiarities, such as word sense comments (SemCor; Landes, Leacock, and Tengi 1998), which correspondingly caused the advancement of similarly explained corpora in different dialects (Bentivogli, Forner, and Pianta 2004; Lupu, Trandabăţ, and Husarciuc 2005; Bond et al. 2012). During this period, etymological comment was in many cases roused by the longing to study a given phonetic peculiarity in huge groups of information, so explanation plots normally mirrored a particular phonetic hypothesis straightforwardly. Fashioners of semantic comment plans zeroed in on deciding the proper classifications and elements to depict the peculiarity being referred to and tried to ignore the possible actual portrayal for the explanations in the asset. To the extent that actual configuration was thought of, the central model for deciding them was constantly the simplicity of handling by programming that would utilize the result. For instance, early arrangements for peculiarities, for example, grammatical feature frequently yield single word per line, isolated from its grammatical feature (POS) label by an exceptional person such as a highlight or a cut (DeRose 1988; Church 1988; see figure 3.1). Syntactic parsers that delivered voting demographic examinations regularly utilized what has come to be known as the

"Penn Treebank design," which sections and homes constituents with brackets, LISPstyle (Marcus, Marcinkiewicz, and Santorini 1993; Charniak 2000; Collins 2003). Reliance parsers frequently utilized a line-based design that gives the syntactic capability also, its contentions in determined fields. Strangely, these early arrangements for POS tagger and parser yield have stayed being used, with very little variety, up to the current day, essentially in the result of POS taggers; see, for instance, the Stanford taggers and parsers for various languages,4

TreeTagger,5 also, TnT.6 Such arrangements depend intensely on void area and line breaks, along with periodic extraordinary characters, to depict components of the investigation (e.g., individual tokens and grammatical feature labels). Subsequently, programming planned to utilize these configurations as information should be modified to comprehend both the importance of these separators and the idea of the data in each field.

The division between calculated content and actual portrayal has not consistently been considered when plans are planned, with conceivably accidental outcomes; for model, a portrayal configuration might force limits on the intricacy of the data that can be incorporated, or could compel the conflation of data into enigmatic names that might be difficult to later unravel. Lately, the need to look at and consolidate explanations, as well as to involve them in programming conditions for which they may have not been initially planned, has expanded, prompting the mindfulness that a calculated plan might be addressed in any of a wide range of actual configurations as well as transduced from one to the next.

Experience with clarified information that is hard to transduce or alter has induced explanation "best practices" that direct that comment data be both express (so it tends to be promptly recovered) and adaptable (so that other data can be subbed or added). As the requirement for dependable programmed explanation for increasingly large collections of information expanded, there in some cases emerged a strain between the prerequisites for precise programmed explanation and a complete etymological bookkeeping that could add to approval and refinement of the basic hypothesis. An early model during the 1990s is the Penn Treebank undertaking's decrease and adjustment of the grammatical feature tagset produced for the Earthy colored Corpus, to get additional exact outcomes from programmed taggers and parsers. In the next many years, AI emerged as the focal technique for NLP; consequently, some explanation projects started to configuration plans gradually, depending on iterative preparation and retraining of learning calculations to foster explanation classes and elements to best tune the plan to the learning task (see, for instance, Pustejovsky and Stubbs 2012) — it might be said moving 180 degrees from deduced conspire configuration in view of hypothesis to deduced conspire improvement in light of information and possibly restricted by imperatives on highlight ID.

Notwithstanding the rising commonness of this approach, there has been little conversation of the effect and worth of iterative plan improvement in the help of machine learning.Over the beyond 30 years, summed up answers for addressing explained language information — that is, arrangements that can apply to an extensive variety of comment types and hence take into consideration joining numerous layers and sorts of semantic data — have been proposed.7 The earliest configuration of note is the Standard Summed up Markup Language (SGML; ISO 8879:1986), which was acquainted in 1986 with empower sharing of machine-clear archives, with no exceptional accentuation on (or even worry for) etymologically explained information. Like its replacement the Extensible Markup Language, or XML (Whinny et al. 2006), SGML characterized a "meta-design" for increasing (importance explaining) electronic reports comprising of rules for isolating markup (labels) from information (by encasing recognizing names in point sections) and furthermore for giving extra data as characteristics (highlights) on those tags.8 SGML likewise determined a setting free language for characterizing labels and the substantial primary relations among them (settling, request, redundancy, and so on) in a SGML Report Type Definition (DTD) that is utilized by SGML-mindful programming to approve the fitting utilization of labels in an adjusting record. XML supplanted the DTD with the XML blueprint, which carries out a similar role as well as some others.

The Text Encoding Drive (TEI)9 Rules, first distributed in 1992, characterized a wide scope of SGML (and, later, XML) follows alongside going with DTDs for encoding language information. Nonetheless, the TEI was from its starting points expected essentially for humanities information and doesn't give rules to addressing numerous peculiarities of interest for phonetic comment. In this manner, during the 1990s, the EU Birds project10 characterized the Corpus Encoding Standard (CES; Ide 1998), a tweaked utilization of the TEI giving a set-up of SGML DTDs for encoding phonetic information and explanations, which was subsequently started up in XML (XCES; Ide, Bonhomme, and Romary 2000).

To a limited extent thus, SGML (what's more, later, XML) started showing up in commented on language information during the mid-1990s — for model, in corpora created in European Association subsidized ventures like PAROLE, information utilized in the US-DARPA Message Grasping Meetings (MUC; Grishman and Sundheim 1995), and the Insider explanation engineering (Grishman 1998) characterized for the NIST Text Recovery Gatherings (TREC),11 which incorporated a CES-based SGML design for trading yield from data extraction undertakings. SGML and XML were moreover taken on by significant explanation structures created during this period, like GATE12 also, NITE,13 for import and commodity of information. Albeit broadly took on, XML as an in-line design for addressing phonetic comments didn't tackle the reusability issue, because of multiple factors.

Above all else, XML expects that in-line labels are organized as a very much framed tree, subsequently denying explanations that structure covering ordered progressions and making lumbering associations between discontiguous segments of the information. Furthermore, similar to all in-line organizes, the addition of explanation data straightforwardly into the information forces etymological understandings that may not be wanted by different clients. This incorporates segmental data — for example, depiction of token limits in-line, whether by encompassing a series of characters with XML labels or by isolating it with void area, line breaks, or other unique characters — as well as the incorporation of explicit comment names and highlights. To take care of this issue, in 1994 the thought of stalemate comment was presented in the CES,14 wherein explanations are kept up with in discrete reports and connected to proper locales of essential information, as opposed to mixed in the essential information or in any case changing them to mirror the aftereffects of handling. This permits different comments for a similar peculiarity to coincide, including variation divisions (e.g., tokenizations), as well as elective investigations created by various processors as well as utilizing different explanation marks and elements.

Comment Charts (AG; Bird and Liberman 2001), presented in 2001, are a deadlock design that addresses comments as names on edges of various autonomous charts characterized over text locales in a record. Since the model was grown essentially with discourse information as a primary concern, the districts are normally characterized between focuses on a course of events, albeit this isn't required. Nonetheless, on the grounds that every comment type or layer is addressed by utilizing a different chart, the AG design isn't appropriate to addressing progressively based peculiarities, for example, syntactic constituency.15 Over the course of the last 10 years, there has been a rising combination of training for addressing semantic explanations in the field, with the points of guaranteeing maximal reusability and furthermore reflecting advances in how we might interpret potential means to best design and coordinate information, particularly Connected Information planned for access and inquiry over the web. Notwithstanding the utilization of stalemate as opposed to in-line comments, the center has moved from recognizing a solitary, general organization to characterizing a fundamental information model for explanations that can empower paltry, coordinated mappings among portrayal designs without loss of data.

The most summed up execution of this approach is the Global Principles Association (ISO) 24612 Etymological Comment Structure (LAF; ISO 24612:2012; Ide and Suderman 2014), which was created throughout the course of recent years to give a thorough and general model for addressing phonetic explanations. To achieve this, LAF was intended to catch the overall standards and practices of both existing furthermore, predicted phonetic explanations, including comments of all media types like message, sound, video, picture, etc, to consider variety in explanation plans, while simultaneously empowering correlation and assessment, converging of various explanations, and improvement of normal apparatuses for making and utilizing clarified information. LAF indicates a bunch of essential design standards, including the unmistakable partition of essential information from comments (i.e., deadlock explanation); division of explanation structure (i.e., actual arrangement) and of explanation content (the classes or names utilized in a comment plan to depict phonetic peculiarities); and a prerequisite that all explanation data be unequivocally addressed instead of building information about the capability of separators, position, and so forth into handling programming. LAF additionally characterized Throughout recent years, what was alluded to as "reusability" in the last part of the 1990s came to be known as "interoperability."

During this period, the requirement for interoperability for etymologically clarified assets turned out to be progressively earnest, as increasingly more language information were being clarified for more than one kind of phonetic peculiarity, and as the need to utilize these comments together was turning out to be more obvious. A trial in the mid-2000s effectively carried the requirement for explanation interoperability to the front, particularly in the US, where it had been less a worry than in Europe: An undertaking financed by the US Public safety Office called for explanation projects at labs around the states to clarify similar information (the 10,000-word Language Figuring out [LU] corpus, or "Boyan 10K") for a wide assortment of etymological peculiarities to concentrate on between level collaborations. The explanations included sentence structure, semantic jobs, assessment, serious conviction, and others. At last, specialists established that it was difficult to consolidate the comments, in light of the fact that of contrasts in designs, names for similar peculiarities, originations of what is a connection furthermore, what is an item, and a deficiency of data implied in the first portrayals while joining was endeavored.

The most outlandish issue was an immense variety in tokenization rehearses, which are frequently negligibly recorded, if by any means. Past these hardships, the meaning of how it affects semantic comments to be interoperable is muddled, yet an unmistakable definition is clearly essential all together both to evaluate the present status of interoperability in the field and to quantify our advancement toward accomplishing interoperability later on. What is required, then, at that point, is a functional definition, which recognizes at least one explicit perceptible circumstances or occasions that can be dependably estimated, and tells where the consequences of the interaction are replicable. In general, can be characterized as a proportion of how much various frameworks, associations, or potentially people can cooperate to accomplish a shared objective. For PC frameworks, interoperability is commonly characterized regarding syntactic interoperability and semantic interoperability. Syntactic interoperability depends on indicated information designs, correspondence conventions, and so forth to guarantee correspondence furthermore, information trade.

The frameworks included can deal with the traded data, yet there is no assurance that the translation is something similar. Semantic interoperability, by contrast, exists when two frameworks can consequently decipher traded data genuinely and precisely and can create helpful outcomes through yielding to a reference model of normal data trade. The substance of the data trade demands is unambiguously characterized: What is sent is equivalent to what is perceived. All the more officially, semantic interoperability of information classes C1 and C2 is the ability of two explanation shoppers to trade comment a1 utilizing C1 and comment a2 utilizing C2 by means of a capability f that maps C1 to C2, with the end goal that an investigation of C2 is indistinguishable from the examination of f(C1); that is, an investigation ought to create a similar outcome for two distinct yet interoperable information classifications. For language assets, the spotlight today is progressively on semantic as opposed to syntactic interoperability. That is, the basic variable supposedly is the exact and predictable translation of traded information, as opposed to the capacity to quickly deal with the information without altering their actual arrangement.

The explanations behind this are a few, on the whole and principal is the presence of a lot of heritage information in a few syntactic organizations, combined with the proceeded with creation of assets addressing phonetic data in differed, yet mappable, ways. Without a doubt, to guarantee interoperability for language assets, the pattern in the field is to determine a theoretical information model for organizing semantic information to which syntactic acknowledge can be planned, along with a planning to a bunch of semantic information classifications that impart the data (phonetic) content. With regards to language assets, then, at that point, we can characterize syntactic interoperability as the capacity of various frameworks to process (read) traded information either straightforwardly or through unimportant change. Semantic interoperability for language assets is basically equivalent to for programming frameworks: It very well may be characterized as the capacity of frameworks to decipher traded semantic data in significant and reliable ways, by reference to a typical arrangement of classes.

Semantic interoperability for etymological comment has shown to be more tricky than syntactic interoperability. As soon as the 1990s, endeavors were dedicated to laying out standard arrangements of information classes, most quite inside the European Birds/ISLE project,19 which created principles for morphosyntax, grammar, subcategorization, text typologies, also, others. Be that as it may, none of these norms has accomplished all inclusive acknowledgment and use. Ongoing enormous scope endeavors tending to normalization of information classes incorporate those inside ISO/TC 37/SC4 (Language Asset The executives), which in 2004 proposed a vault obliging the requirements of phonetic comment (Ide and Romary 2004) and in this way carried out ISOcat (Kemps-Snijders et al. 2009), a web-based vault that is available and extensible with new information classes by the local area.

As of late, the ISOcat classifications pertinent for etymological comment were relocated to the CLARIN

Information Idea Registry.20 Different endeavors incorporate OLiA (Chiarcos 2012), a storehouse of explanation phrasing for different etymological peculiarities planned to apply across various dialects, furthermore, the Internet Administration Trade Jargon (Ide et al. 2014b) being worked on inside the Language Applications (LAPPS) Framework project (Ide et al. 2014a). Regardless of these rehashed endeavors, right now no generally acknowledged set of classifications exists, nor does even settlement on what the classifications ought to be.

In any case, some agreement has been reached, essentially among plans deliberately customized to address the issues of normal NLP apparatuses, which depend on a few moderately normal practices that have developed throughout the long term. These shared characteristics ordinarily allude to credit types, for example, "part-ofspeech," "constituent," "semantic job," and "connection" and leave open the scope of legitimate values. This maintains a strategic distance from a portion of the nastier sorts of planning issues by pushing off issues of harmonization among explicit qualities to one more stage or component; for test ple, instruments might be expected to give metadata about the organized tagsets they input and/ or on the other hand yield (e.g., the Penn Treebank grammatical form labels or the PropBank plan of semantic job task) that can be checked for consistency at runtime. Different sorts of explanation have a genuinely predictable (or possibly effectively mappable) set of classifications, for example, nounchunk and verbchunk, coreference (specifies, delegate), normal subsets of named elements (individual, association, area, date), conditions (head, subordinate, etc. In any case, full agreement on phonetic classifications and values is probably not going to be accomplished whenever before long, if by any means. Likewise with syntactic interoperability, the best way might be to track down means to permit adaptability while keeping up with the capacity to plan among classifications. End As of now, there is union inside the local area of different means to accomplish explanation interoperability and an overall eagerness to seek after and guarantee such means. In any case, it is challenging to recognize an undeniable arrangement or even a make way to continue in request to accomplish it completely.

New advancements will probably arise that might influence the way we move toward the interoperability issue, much as the advancement of the Semantic Web and its supporting RDF/OWL design have affected information models for explanations over the past fifteen years. Meanwhile, the trudging progress in quest for interoperability that has been made throughout the course of recent many years will keep, crawling toward an answer that is at this point just indirectly noticeable.

4. Linguistic Linked Open Data and Under-Resourced Languages From Collection to Application

expanded action in studios, summer schools, and datathons, including the First Studio on Coordinated effort and Figuring for Under-Resourced Dialects in the Connected Open Information Time (CCURL-2014, Reykjavik, Iceland, May 2014), the Main Summer Datathon on Etymological Connected Open Information (SD-LLOD 2015, Madrid, Spain, June 2015), the EUROLAN-2015 summer school on Etymological Connected Open Information (Sibiu, Romania, July 2015), and the LSA Summer Foundation studio on the Improvement of Etymological Connected Open Information (LLOD) Assets for Cooperative Information Concentrated Exploration in the Language Sciences (LLOD-LSA 2015, Chicago, July 2015).

Since the utilizations of Connected Information to language assets are complex (Chiarcos, Nordhoff, and Hellmann 2012), a comprehensive and cutting-edge review is past degree for our commitment in this part. We hence take a specific spotlight on a unique exploration issue in semantics — that is, the examination of under-resourced dialects; we delineate the capability of Connected Information for measurable methodologies in typology and cross-etymological multivariate techniques for exploring overall etymological and social variety. This includes managing the accompanying inquiries: • How might cooperative methodologies and advances be productively applied to the turn of events and sharing of assets for under-resourced dialects? • How might little language assets be reused proficiently and successfully, reach bigger crowds, and be coordinated into applications? • How could these assets be put away, uncovered, and got to by end clients and applications?

How might investigate on under-resourced dialects benefit from Semantic Web innovations, and explicitly the Connected Information structure? In this section, we contend for the advantages of making and utilizing Connected Information. Specifically, Connected Information is a productive technique for accomplishing interoperability and making valuable information spreads of under-resourced dialects. A large number of these dialects are spoken in regions as of late entered by innovation, for example, mobile phones, and this makes more information and in this manner more financial open doors for individuals utilizing them. To begin with, we characterize what we mean by "under-resourced dialects." Then, at that point, we give a brief, nontechnical prologue to Connected Information and we home in on involving Connected Information for etymological purposes.

Then, we give two short contextual investigations that delineate the expanded a chance for coordinated effort while making under-resourced language information and instruments utilizing Connected Information advances. Later we portray an enormous in-progress cooperative dataset, the Semantic Connected Open Information cloud (LLOD), and we present the Open Phonetics Working Gathering (OWLG), a development drove both by PC researchers and etymologists pointed toward expanding the cooperative energy between research being finished in limited scope circles (e.g., field laborers and limited scope language documentation projects) and bigger and frequently undertaking driven drives like MLODE or LIDER5 to help content examination of unstructured multilingual information.

We start by depicting why expanded admittance to under-resourced dialects is significant. Furthermore, we end with headings to extra data on Semantic Connected Open Information, including a few DIY rules. What Are Under-Resourced Dialects? Etymological Variety Despite the fact that our view is exceptionally distant from complete, overall semantic variety is just bewildering (cf. Evans and Levinson 2009).6 Given the condition of the world's dialects, large numbers of which are either jeopardized or moribund,7 it is a high need to record and depict these dialects. In view of this image, one more reality to remember is the absence of information that would empower us to attempt wide quantitative examinations on cross-etymological variety. Typologists have adapted by utilizing factual examining strategies to derive qualities from signals in the genealogical plunge or areal contact between dialects (Cysouw 2005).

This absence of information on the world's dialects is alluded to as the bibliographic testing inclination. The World Chart book of Language Designs (WALS; Dryer and Haspelmath 2013) is a work of art model, essentially among typologists, of a comfort test with more than 150 factors, models being "Word Request" and "Hand and Arm," that essentially illustrates overall etymological variety, which thus spikes subjective or speculative clarifications (McNew, Derungs, and Moran 2018). The most itemized picture that exists with respect to the semantic documentation of the world's dialects is the Glottolog (Nordhoff et al. 2013).8 Glottolog contains a catalog about what is as of now had some significant awareness of the condition of documentation of the world's dialects and it is accessible as Connected Information (Hammarström et al. 2015).

Be that as it may, what is known about the documentation of the world's "under-resourced" dialects, and how does Connected Information assist us with joining that information with previously existing information? Under-Resourced Dialects Obviously dialects without any documentation at all are "under-resourced," since they are essentially not resourced, in a manner of speaking. There is, in any case, an idea that there is a bunch of dialects somewhere close to insignificantly recorded ones (say, one syntax or word reference) and enormous proven and factual dialects (models being Chinese, English, French, German, Russian, and Spanish). This arrangement of dialects has been given different marks in the writing. Maybe the most established is "low-thickness dialects" (Jones and Havrilla 1998). The expressions "medium-thickness" and "lower-thickness dialects" have additionally been begat (e.g., Maxwell and Hughes 2006). The last option term explicitly alludes to "how much computational assets accessible, instead of the quantity of speakers any given language could have" (Maxwell and Hughes 2006; Meyers et al. 2007).

How much available information, paying little heed to languagIn the language asset local area, different classifications of "under-resourced" or "pitifully upheld" dialects have been utilized: 1. Absence of admittance to language information — a general absence of language documentation and depiction (no sentence structures, word references, or corpora) 2. Absence of admittance to advanced language information — assets exist yet can only with significant effort be gotten to 3. Absence of IT/NLP support 4. Restricted interoperability of information and apparatuses For class 1, there are large number of dialects with negligible or no documentation at all. This reality is obvious to such an extent that we really want not list examples.

Class 2 applies to dialects for which materials exist yet admittance to those materials is preposterous. In the most fundamental case, there is an absence of admittance to a computerized asset; for case, some etymologist made a corpus of language X utilizing programming Y that is currently outdated. Maybe more regularly, the instance of detachment is because of different elements, like unsupported person encodings, inaccessible textual styles, the absence of a normalized orthography, or just blocked off information (brought about by copyright limitations, since they are housed in confidential assortments, or a couple of paper duplicates exist, etc). For sound and video information, the nontransformation from simple to advanced (or future) designs, as occurred with first reel-to-reel and afterward tape tapes, frustrates information access.

Class 3 of under-resourced language information is just applicable when the initial two focuses have been tended to. Without confined computerized information, language-explicit IT/NLP applications can't exist. In such manner, we see solidly where under-resourced dialects lie, with respect to model the Hausa language which, with about 30 to 50 million speakers, doesn't have the advanced assets required for doing essential Normal Language Handling (NLP) undertakings. Class 4 leads us to the last issue in characterizing under-resourced dialects. Mechanically, restricted interoperability of information and devices is predominant in numerous areas, like apparatuses also, explanations, which utilize various organizations and shows. As of not long ago, the Russian language has been a great representation; regardless of being spoken by ~150 million individuals around the world, it has as of not long ago needed huge scope corpora, comment plans, and exploratory NLP devices .

Since the distribution of the syntactic comments of the Russian Public Corpus12 in 2008, the circumstance is gradually getting to the next level. However, even the ongoing absence of interoperable computerized assets for creating NLP instruments embodies the point about under-resourced dialects raised by Maxwell and Hughes (2006): It is the absence of open advanced information, not the number of inhabitants in speakers of a given language, that decides if the language is under-resourced. Etymological Assets Deciding under-resourced dialects according to a computational point of view requires that the assets of a given language be measured. In such manner, the METANET white papers (Rehm and Uszkoreit 2013) have summed up the status (in general) formally recognizede-speaker amounts, is the subject that ties these different terms together.

dialects in the European Association (EU). The image isn't especially fulfilling. Out of 30 dialects, just English is named having great help with regards to language assets. As far as language assets expected by various subfields of NLP, a portion of the EU dialects have fragmentary support.

And just five EU public dialects are said to have powerless or no help in such resources.14 Inclusion is significantly more grim inside specific NLP subfields; for instance, 66% of the dialects have feeble to-no help for machine interpretation. Obviously this is the NLP view, where the level of asset support is assessed from specialists' evaluation of both the quality/size of advanced text, discourse, and equal corpora and their explanations, and of the quality/inclusion of machine-coherent lexical assets and sentence structures. Asset types embraced to characterize a language as being (under-)resourced in etymology are to some degree unique.

Glottolog, for instance, covers the known language documentation with an emphasis on syntaxes, punctuation representations, word references, and wordlists. These assets for the most part accompanied subjective investigations, that is to say, examinations composed by language specialists on the premise of specific hypothetical previously established inclinations. Naturally, the demonstration of making a depiction of a language forces hypothetical requirements on the material gathered. As such, no generally acknowledged hypothesis exists for depicting a language as a framework or a model, thus these language assets, in any event, when electronically accessible, are frequently not accessible in a machine-clear arrangement and in any occasion are normally contradictory with one another.

Comparable interoperability issues exist between these assets and clarified corpora, with regard to machine-coherent word references and syntaxes expected by the METANET meaning of "pitifully upheld" dialects. In any case, a few phonetic information structures have as a matter of fact been normalized, to different degrees. We center around lexical assets and explained (corpus/gleam) information. The third major class of computerized language assets — instruments for mechanized and semiautomated explanation — is past the extent of this part, as it surmises the accessibility of word references or corpora. Lexical Assets: Wordlists and Word references The wordlist is in many cases considered the most fundamental semantic information structure. This speculation is shallow and misses the way that the wordlist might be more complicated than a basic sets of words with names, for example, "sparkle" and "word.

" Yet the topic of what a gleam is, is significant in characterizing the idea of the connection among "sparkle" and "word." Maybe better characterized considering multilingual wordlists is the thought of a "idea" that guides to a specific language-explicit structure. For instance, numerous dialects breakdown the ideas of "hand" and "arm" (utilized by English speakers, for instance) into one idea that is a single element. Consequently, there is a planning connection between specific ideas, as conceptualized in various dialects, and their language-explicit structures. The connection between idea and structure is neither a definition nor an interpretation, but instead what has been named "partner" in multilingual near settings (Great 2013).15 A word reference is more point by point than a wordlist. It is normally glorified as an assortment of formto-meaning depictions.

Portrayals of structures are normally determined in socially unambiguoussettings (like neighborhood greenery), which makes it hard to consolidate various word references (or on the other hand vocabularies) into one enormous similar multilingual source, similar to a multilanguage wordlist. For dialects that need physically delivered language assets however that accompany significant measures of carefully accessible text, one more kind of lexical asset can be referenced: recurrence and collocation ("affiliation") word references that can be naturally gotten from running text (Zock and Bilac 2004).

One model is the Wortschatz portal,16 which gives collocation and recurrence word references for 229 dialects, including minor dialects, for example, Manx (terminated), Neo-Aramaic (jeopardized), or Klingon (fictitious). Figure 4.1 shows the model section Deitsch "German" from Pennsylvania Dutch (a German lingo spoken in the US) alongside the data gave about it: recurrence class (to gauge whether it is has linguistic or lexical capability), models, co-happening words and regular collocations, including expressions of a similar semantic class (Englisch, Dutch, Schprooch "language"), related ethnic and geographic ideas (Pennsylvania, Pennsilfaanisch, Mennonites), and related action words (of talking, kenne "to be aware," lanne "to learn," schwetze "to talk").

Albeit this data doesn't supplant that in a conventional word reference, it tends to be utilized as an instrument to build one, or to affirm the use of an obscure word (Benson 1990). These assets are additionally helpful for bootstrapping the improvement of multilingual lexical information interpretation charts (cf. Kamholz, Pool, and Colowick 2014). Commented on Information: Sparkles and Corpora In phonetically explained information, models are commonly given as interlinear sparkled text (IGT), a semi-normalized information structure containing at least three lines that prototypically contain three things: a particular record, a point by point semantic understanding, (for example, a morphological sparkle or a grammatical feature tag), and an exacting translation.17 After recognizable proof (say, by means of normal articulations), IGT is consequently extricated from sites and online archives and afterward relegated an ISO 639-3:2007 language name identifier, got from ascribes distinguished in the source record. Looking across IGT of thousands of dialects in changing subtlety is attractive, yet since the record furthermore, explanation styles might vary from one record to another, some extra layer of what might be called an ontological explanation is expected to intelligently and reliably characterize relations in the dataset (cf. Moran 2012a).

Made a stride further, the rule of gleaming has been stretched out to the comment of bigger texts and, surprisingly, whole corpora, concerning example by utilizing apparatuses like Toolbox.18 By plan, corpora are organized substances comprising of assortments of essential information (messages, records, picture, sound, or video content), along with their metadata (creator, source, date, area, language), and, generally, etymological explanations also. Present day corpora have been utilized as a device for etymological examination since the Earthy colored Corpus (Kučera and Francis 1967), which has since been gathered as a reference base for the American Legacy Word reference, and which all the more as of late turned into a foundation of corpus phonetics and NLP with the Penn Treebank (Taylor, Marcus, and Santorini 2003) and others.

Accepting the Penn Treebank for instance, ordinary explanations contain lemmatization, morphosyntax (grammatical forms, inflectional morphology), syntactic investigations (here express structure syntax, generally likewise ostensible/clausal pieces or reliance investigation), and, for well-resourced dialects, more significant levels of examination like semantic jobs (Kingsbury furthermore, Palmer 2002; Meyers, Reeves, Macleod, Szekely, et al. 2004), transient relations (Pustejovsky et al. 2003), pragmatics (Carlson et al. 2002; Prasad et al. 2008), or co-reference (Pradhan et al. 2007) — for this situation particular subcorpora of the Penn Treebank. Figure 4.2 shows morphosyntactic and syntactic comments of the Penn Treebank.19 For dialects without explained corpora, equal corpora (like the Holy book, the Qur'an, different deciphered writing, specialized or functional manuals, confinement documents from programming circulations, or captions) can be utilized to bootstrap etymological comments by means of explanation projection (Yarowsky,

Ngai, and Wicentowski 2001). Adjusted syntactic explanations in an equal corpus are displayed in figure 4.3

For dialects with a lot of carefully accessible text, yet inadequate with regards to NLP support, solo NLP devices might be a choice. These broaden the idea of collocation extraction to unaided linguistic investigation (Clark 2003). Nonetheless, as this data is just to some degree interpretable regarding customary syntactic classifications, and requires significant measures of information, this is a momentum subject of exploration and past the extent of this part. Summing up, the designs of phonetic assets are complex even inside a solitary language, and for under-resourced dialects asset improvement even requires joins between such organized elements across various dialects. Asset incorporation is in this manner not just a vital issue for current etymology overall yet additionally for under-resourced dialects specifically. Asset Incorporation It is essential to take note of that semantic assets are perplexing and organized elements that are made out of various parts that should be incorporated assuming interoperability is to be achieved.

For instance, there is essential information (like lexemes in a word reference, message in a corpus, sound or video transfers in mixed media corpora), optional information (counting normal language interpretations, like sparkles and their definitions in a word reference, or the interpretation in an equal corpus or a bilingual wordlist), linguistic examinations (like in word references, shines, and comments), and potentially cross-references, (for example, a watchword in-setting [KWIC] view in a corpus, a query office from corpus to word reference to look at the meaning of a word, or a query office from word reference to corpus to give true models). Out of this present circumstance of inoperability of information sources and types arises the test to address (etymological) information structures on a specialized level. Changing answers for the issue have been proposed, however they have frequently either been issue explicit (say, a space explicit [lexicon] XML design through Tool kit) or what may be classified "nearby" (that is, mix inside a social data set, telling for example the best way to store language and creator explicit IGT models). Every arrangement likely has its benefits; the most commonly realized arrangements have accomplished a degree of development or exposure that has prompted their acknowledgment inside their local area.

All things considered, semantic assets made in a peculiar style are not effectively reused, except if they can be (effectively) incorporated with other datasets. This is one of the center functionalities of Connected Information. And yet, Connected Information assists us with beating the heterogeneity of existing formalisms for various neighborhood assets, like word references and corpora. Notwithstanding, existing foundations, assets, and apparatuses will keep on being utilized, and it would be untimely to recommend a general shift from existing innovation to Connected Information. All things considered, we outline here ways that might be utilized to naturally switch a current asset over completely to Connected Information and exhibit a portion of the advantages we have gathered from this change. To sum up, inquiries of how etymological information types are changed into Connected Information are all around as eccentric as the tasks or individuals who pursue the plan choices to change over from, say, a phonetic information type A to the Connected Information execution B.

We start with a brief outline of Connected Information and afterward we show how a few datasets have been changed over into Connected Information in the Etymological Connected Open Information (LLOD) cloud. Connected Information and Under-Resourced Language Information Connected Information Connected Information are a bunch of rules, or "best practices," maybe, for distributing information on the web. Connected Information incorporates a bunch of conventions and guidelines, the reason for which is to lay out joins between various datasets. Joins are utilized here comprehensively; systems give pervasive URI goal whether a client taps on a connection in their program, or whether PC code naturally creeps through machine interpretable information. The Connected Open Information worldview hypothesizes four standards for the distribution and portrayal of web assets: 1. Alluded elements ought to be assigned by utilizing URIs. 2. These URIs ought to be resolvable over HTTP.

Information ought to be addressed through W3C guidelines (like RDF; see underneath). 4. An asset ought to incorporate connections to different assets. These standards work with data combination, and in this way, interoperability, in that they expect elements to be tended to in a universally unambiguous manner (rule 1 over), that they can be gotten to (rule 2) and deciphered (rule 3), and that substances that are related on a calculated level are likewise truly connected with one another (rule 4). Connected Information is additionally centered around data coordination, and specifically on underlying also, theoretical interoperability. Connected Information designers take a stab at primary interoperability to achieve practically identical configurations and conventions to get to both their own and others' information. An objective is to utilize a similar inquiry language for various datasets, which the client can question across, no matter what controlling the basic rationale (or "semantics") encoded into the (consolidated) dataset(s) (cf. Moran 2012b).

In the meaning of Connected Information, the Asset Portrayal Structure (RDF) gets exceptional consideration. RDF was intended to give metadata about assets that are accessible either disconnected (as in books in a library) or on the web (digital books in a store). RDF gives a nonexclusive information model in light of named coordinated charts, which can be serialized in various designs. Data is communicated with regards to significantly increases — comprising of a predicate (connection, i.e., a named edge) that associates a subject (i.e., an asset as a marked hub) with its item (i.e., another asset or a strict or string). For instance, the assertion Christian Chiarcos realizes Steven Moran may be (pseudo)- encoded as a solitary string comprising of the subject, predicate, and item triple: Subject http://www.acoli.informatik.uni-frankfurt.de/~chiarcos Predicate http://xmlns.com/foaf/0.1/knows Object http://www.comparativelinguistics.uzh.ch/de/moran.html As displayed, RDF assets (nodes)21 are addressed by Uniform Asset Identifiers (URIs), and they are consequently around the world unambiguous in the Snare of Information (as well as the "Semantic Web"). Connected Information framework permits assets facilitated at various areas to allude to one another, which thus makes an organization of assortments of information whose components are thickly interlaced. A few linearizations for RDF information exist, which contrast in comprehensibility and conservativeness. RDF/XML was the first norm for that reason, however it has been generally supplanted by Turtle, a more comprehensible organization. In Turtle, significantly increases are composed as groupings of subject, predicate, and item parts, finished up with a last spot. . A more minimized portrayal can be accomplished utilizing namespace prefixes rather than full URIs: PREFIX acoli: PREFIX cluzh: PREFIX foaf: acoli:chiarcos foaf:knows cluzh:moran .

A few information base executions for RDF information are accessible, and these can be gotten to utilizing SPARQL (Prud'hommeaux and Seaborne 2008), a normalized inquiry language for RDF information. SPARQL utilizes a triple documentation like Turtle, where properties and RDF assets can be supplanted by factors. SPARQL was roused by Organized Question Language (SQL), in which factors can be presented in a different SELECT block, and in which imperatives on these factors are communicated in a WHERE block in a triple documentation. In this way, for instance, we can question for relations between two specific individuals: SELECT ?connection WHERE { acoli:chiarcos ?connection cluzh:moran . } SPARQL doesn't just help running questions against individual RDF information bases that are open over HTTP (supposed SPARQL endpoints), however it likewise permits clients to consolidate data from numerous stores (known as "organization"). RDF can accordingly be utilized both to lay out an organization (or haze) of information assortments, and to straightforwardly inquiry that organization. Along these lines, Connected Information works with the asset availability and reusability on various levels (Ide and Pustejovksy 2010): How to get to (read) an asset? (Underlying interoperability) Assets utilize tantamount formalisms to address and to get to information (designs, conventions, question dialects, and so on), so they can be gotten to in a uniform manner and that their data can be coordinated with one another. How to decipher (figure out) data from an asset? (Applied interoperability) Assets share a typical jargon, so semantic data from one asset can be settled against data from another asset, e.g., syntactic portrayals can be connected to a wording vault.

How to incorporate (blend) data from various assets? (Organization) Web assets are given such that remote access is upheld. Utilizing basically interoperable portrayals, a question language with league support permits the client to run inquiries against various outer assets inside a solitary question, and in this way to coordinate their data at question time. At the end of the day, underlying interoperability implies that assets can be gotten to in a uniform manner and that their data can be coordinated with one another. Calculated interoperability is the objective to create and (re-)utilize shared vocabularies for comparable ideas. Shared vocabularies permit the client to run a similar inquiry across various datasets.

Theoretical interoperability, additionally alluded to as semantic interoperability, goes past utilizing bound together underlying information organizes and gives a kind of mark interpretation with an extra layer of Portrayal Rationales, concerning model while utilizing OWL-DL to encode datasets.22 Once more, to make information basically and thoughtfully interoperable (to shifting degrees), the term organization alludes to bringing fundamentally and reasonably interoperable datasets together on the web — distributing information previously distributed on the web, ideally under an open permit and with an inquiry point of interaction like a SPARQL endpoint.

Open information is essential for the mission of the Open Phonetics Working Gathering (OWLG), which we depict later in this part. To start with, we feature the information incorporation issue and afterward we talk about Connected Information with regards to under-resourced language information and NLP. Under-Resourced Language Information The devices used to deliver language information and to make and disperse nitty gritty (and frequently computationally implemented)23 phonetic examinations produce a quickly expanding sum also, profundity of inoperable datasets. The broadness and profundity of progressing research projects range from some limited scale, single-researcher information assortment projects (as in "language specialist X works with the final speaker of language Y") to more modest to-medium-scale corpora assortments (say, a 1,000,000 word corpus of X), to bigger to-medium ventures that consolidate numerous assets, (for example, CLLD),24 to huge scope enormous information delivering endeavors (Wiktionary, DBPedia, and so forth).

Albeit the focal point of each undertaking varies, every one of them gain from more or more extravagant information sources. Among many, prominent instances of assortments that contain nitty gritty information on under-resourced language information incorporate the ANU Data set (Donohue et al. 2013), AUTOTYP (Bickel and Nichols 2015), STEDT (Matisoff 2015), and PHOIBLE (Moran, McCloy, and Wright 2014). A gigantic measure of exertion has been placed into making these rich datasets, which are frequently pointed toward gathering phonetic variety. Each dataset contains sets of dialects that are underresourced, however those information stay in project-explicit configurations, bringing about deficient information access, opportunities for sharing, and mix for inquiry and examination. Connected Information for Semantics and NLP For clients wishing to make Connected Information for semantics, we note that distributing Connected Information permits assets to be internationally and extraordinarily recognized to such an extent that they can be recovered through standard web conventions. In addition, assets can be handily connected to each other in a uniform design and consequently become fundamentally interoperable.

The five fundamental advantages of Connected Information for phonetics and NLP can be expressed as follows (Chiarcos et al. 2013): Reasonable interoperability: Semantic Web advances permit clients to give, to keep up with, and to share unified, yet openly available wording stores. Reference to such wording storehouses works with reasonable interoperability, since various ideas utilized in the explanation are upheld by remotely given definitions; these normal definitions might be utilized for examination or data coordination across heterogeneous assets. Connecting through URIs: URIs give around the world unambiguous identifiers, and assuming assets are open over HTTP making resolvable references to URIs is conceivable. Various assets created by free examination gatherings can be associated into a haze of assets.

Data mix at inquiry runtime (Alliance): Alongside HTTP-open archives and resolvable URIs, it is feasible to consolidate data from truly isolated storehouses in a solitary question at runtime; indeed, assets can be exceptionally recognized and effectively referred to from some other asset on the web through URIs. Like hyperlinks in the HTML web, the supposed Trap of Information made by these connections considers route along these associations, and accordingly permits free coordination of data from various assets in the cloud. Dynamic import: When phonetic assets are interlinked by references to resolvable URIs rather than framework characterized IDs (or static duplicates of parts from another asset), one ought to constantly give admittance to the latest variant of an asset. For example, for local area kept up with phrasing vaults like the ISO TC 37/SC 4 Information Classification Vault (ISOcat; Windhouwer and Wright 2012; Wright 2004), new classifications, definitions, or models can be presented once in a while, and this data is accessible promptly to anybody whose assets allude to ISOcat URIs. To protect connect consistency among Etymological Connected Open Information (LLOD) assets, notwithstanding, it is emphatically encouraged to apply a legitimate forming framework to such an extent that regressive similarity can be safeguarded: Adding ideas or models is unproblematic, yet when ideas are erased, renamed, or on the other hand reclassified, another rendition ought to be given. Biological system: RDF as an information trade structure is kept up with by an interdisciplinary, enormous, and dynamic local area, and it accompanies a created framework that gives APIs, data set executions, specialized help, and validators for different RDF-based dialects, like reasoners for OWL.

For engineers of etymological assets, this biological system can offer mechanical help or off-the-rack executions for normal issues; for instance, an information base can be created to be equipped for supporting adaptable, diagram based information structures as important for multi-facet corpora (Ide and Suderman 2007).To these, we might add that the conveyed approach of the Connected Information worldview works with the circulated improvement of a trap of assets. It likewise gives a component to joint effort between analysts who use information, utilizing shared sets of innovations. One result is the rise of interdisciplinary endeavors to make huge and interconnected sets of assets in etymology — and then some.

These advantages are of specific significance to less-resourced dialects. Through later local area endeavors, for example, the OWLG and the development of the LLOD cloud, assets from numerous dialects can now be: • tracked down through focal metadata storehouses (for the OWLG DataHub), • gotten to by crossing starting with one asset then onto the next that is connected with it, and • distinguished and reported through a bunch of shared vocabularies It is vital to note right now that the simple accessibility of semantic assets may as of now further develop opportunities for finding as well as really creating assets for extra under-resourced dialects. For instance, NLP devices, explanations, and machine-decipherable vocabularies might be ported starting with one language then onto the next, related one.

This probably won't help language confines, like Basque or maybe Etruscan, however it would significantly advance the circumstance of, say, Faroese on the off chance that assets from Icelandic can be ported. A comparative circumstance continues for the Bantu dialects in Africa, for which a specific level of NLP support has been accomplished exclusively in the country of South Africa, though Bantu dialects in most different nations further north have no help by any means. In specific regards, these dialects are moderately firmly related, with the goal that asset porting between dialects might be a choice.

Models for such porting approaches incorporate the examination of Ugaritic (an old Semitic language spoken in the second millenium BCE) through assets initially produced for the morphological examination of Hebrew (Snyder, Barzilay, and Knight 2010) or then again for ways to deal with performing character-based interpretation between related dialects, concerning model with orthography being "standardized" from a less-resourced language to another; the apparatus chain created for the last option case can be applied to the previous (Moran 2009; Tiedemann 2012). As a formalism to give language assets in a basically furthermore, reasonably interoperable way, Connected Information gives a possible foundation to future methodologies on asset porting across differing dialects and areas. Contextual investigations In characterizing under-resourced dialects, we referenced four key issues:

(1) absence of admittance to language information,

(2) absence of admittance to advanced information,

 (3) absence of IT/NLP support, and

(4) restricted interoperability of information and devices.

We can expect to expand the restricted interoperability of information and instruments by working on both the reasonable and underlying interoperability of existing information sources. This can be attempted with expanded IT/NLP support among dialects and activities, which can thus be utilized to direct digitization endeavors to (somewhat) make up for the absence of lexical assets of under-resourced dialects. Endeavors to further develop theoretical and underlying interoperability are exemplified by shared vocabularies; models incorporate Vocabulary Model for Ontologies (lemon;

McCrae et al. 2010; McCrae, Spohr, and Cimiano 2011; vocabularies), Lexvo25 (de Melo 2015) and Glottolog26 (Hammarström et al. 2015; language recognizable proof), PHOIBLE Online27 (Moran, McCloy, furthermore, Wright 2014; phonemes), and OLiA (Chiarcos 2008; comments). Different endeavors to increment the absence of lexical assets are exemplified by projects like QuantHistLing (see underneath), PanLex28 (Kamholz, Pool, and Colowick 2014), and LiODi.29 In this segment we give models as brief contextual investigations. QuantHistLing Projects like QuantHistLing (Quantitative Authentic Linguistics)30 outline the work expected to make etymologically different examples of lexical information accessible to an expansive and computationally keen crowd. Any task should initially distinguish the phonetic information sources (like wordlists and word references) that it wishes to utilize or to make.

QuantHistLing has digitized around 200 source records, the greater part of them accessible just on paper and a considerable lot of them the sole assets accessible for the inadequately portrayed and under-resourced dialects that they depict. Two models, one of a near wordlist and the other of a bilingual word reference, separately, are displayed in figure 4.4. The digitization pipeline includes changing printed sources into electronic sources (whether by OCR or by manual composing). When sources exist in an electronic structure, for word references the fascinating pieces of every section are distinguished, commonly with source-explicit normal articulations, to extricate head words, interpretations, model sentences, and part-ofspeech data. For wordlists, ideas and their gleams are separated.

Stalemate explanations might be added to the information by project individuals; for instance, the "dictinterpretation" information type is added by project individuals and may incorporate manual revisions or other relevant data. The QuantHistLing project delivers a straightforward information yield design that contains metadata (prefixed with the image "@") and tab-delimited lexical result on a source-bysource basis.31 A model is given in figure 4.5. Utilizing the comma-isolated values (CSV) information as information, a straightforward content was composed to change the information into RDF.

A RDF model that is determined in the Dictionary Model for Ontologies (lemon; McCrae et al. 2010; McCrae, Spohr, and Cimiano 2011) was made for the QuantHistLing information (Moran and Brümmer 2013). Lemon is an ontological model for displaying vocabularies and machine-clear word references for connecting to both the Semantic Web furthermore, the Connected Information cloud. The QuantHistLing-lemon model is shown in figure 4.6. Given the objectives of QuantHistLing to uncover and explain phylogenetic connections between dialects, the change of wordlist information and of word reference information from various source reports to a RDF chart gives scientists a basically

interoperable asset that we call an interpretation chart — a RDF model that permits clients to question across the basic vocabularies and word references to separate semantically adjusted wordlists through their sparkles and translations.32 Distinguishing semantically related sets of words from various dialects is one stage in exploring the authentic development of dialects and their conceivable relatedness.33 Change of wordlist and word reference information from QuantHistLing into lemon has the advantage that lemon is firmly incorporated with Semantic Web innovations.

Specifically, lexical information in lemon are effectively made interoperable with the Etymological Connected Open Information (LLOD) cloud. In this way, the subsequent lexical asset is accessible on the web in a norm design and open, the information can be made inquiry capable by means of a SPARQL endpoint,34 and the utilization of the lemon metaphysics with Connected Information helps QuantHistLing in its objectives to combine dissimilar word reference and wordlist information through semantic sense and importance mappings into an philosophy for diagram to-CSV extraction of multilingual and unique resources.35 This is characteristic of analysts' endeavors at changing multilingual lexical datasets into Semantic Web information.

That is, there exists a few info information design (frequently CSV) from which lexical semantic information should be planned to comparative hubs in a given interpretation diagram. Moreover, metadata about dialects or assets in the dataset should be clarified with URIs so those assets can be connected to other datasets. This connecting lies at the core of the Connected Information drive, and specifically of the LLOD, which expects to make accessible a rising number of assets on under-resourced dialects to explore networks through the web. PHOIBLE in CLLD The PHOIBLE data set is a wide assortment of communicated in dialects' phonological systems.

It encodes a hypothesis of semantic depiction that incorporates frameworks of phonemes, allophones, and their phonological molding conditions. The formalism is known as particular element hypothesis, is semi-double, and has been utilized to display wide base applications for programmed communicated in language (even vernacular) acknowledgment. Particular element hypothesis in phonology was created in the ahead of schedule to-mid-twentieth hundred years as a reflection of the actual acoustic signs (in discourse) into a graphemic-based encoding (that is, letter-based record) of sounds and their differentiations. This hypothesis permits language specialists to portray and anticipate (un)natural classes of sound changes. PHOIBLE was at first distributed as Connected Information in a basic RDF model, which incorporates ideas (dialects, sounds, and highlights) and the relationsbetween dialects furthermore, their endlessly sounds and their elements (Moran 2012a, 2012b). This model was made by prearranging input in CSV information and yielding a RDF chart, given a model, into a XML serialization.

All the more as of late, the PHOIBLE information has been integrated into the Cross-Phonetic Connected Information (CLLD) system (Forkel 2014). For under-resourced dialects, the CLLD system gives a few clear instruments to taking organized information (say, CSV and BibTeX for bibliographic references), particularly from different etymology datasets like typological databases,37 and producing end-userfriendly interacts with highlights like explorable guides, sortable elements, and accessible content.38 Past a decent web interface, CLLD applications give their information as Connected Information portrayed with VoID portrayals, and those information are available through instruments, for example, rdflib39 and Python.40 The center CLLD information model is outlined in figure 4.7, which contains ideas (Dataset, Language, Boundary, ValueSet, Worth, Unit, UnitParameter, UnitValue, Source, Sentence, Commitment) and the relations between substances — giving a triples model (Forkel 2014).

The effect of CLLD applications is explained in Forkel (2014). In aggregate, questions like "give me all data on language X" are conceivable, and they will return all data from all CLLD applications for a given language. The question usefulness likewise considers testing guesses made specifically sources, like the WALS section "Hand and Arm" (Brown 2013), on the development of dialects and different parts of etymological variety. More complex questions that unify the CLLD assets are likewise conceivable through the CLLD Portal.42 Extricated information can then be utilized either to seed or to extend the improvement of other datasets with language metadata, phonetic elements, and lexical and orthographic encoded information — specifically, information on under-resourced dialects that might be utilized in virtual entertainment outlets like informal communities, sites, or tweets.

Joining Contextual analyses We have previously introduced two brief contextual investigations of the change of phonetic information into Connected Information. Presently we might ask, how could we at any point manage these subsequent Connected Information assets? One thought is that we should reexamine the idea of asset porting through character-based machine interpretation. For instance, utilizing the PHOIBLE jargon, we can depict dialects fair and square of their phonemic design and, consequently, we can likewise portray the precise sound correspondences between various dialects. We have a suitable objective dataset in QuantHistLing.

Right now, character-based machine interpretation figures out how to recognize relating characters or character gatherings, yet regards them as murky signs. As a matter of fact, nonetheless, sound correspondences will generally reflect precise regulations, implying that not one explicit phoneme formed into another, however that all phonemes with a particular component transformed into phonemes whose component esteem was supplanted by another worth. Dissimilar to cutting edge character-based models, a phoneme-level model would have the option to catch this data if a planning from character to phoneme (or phonetic list of capabilities) can be established.

This is, in any case, a course for future examination, and it requires a nearby coordination of etymological and NLP skill. Under the umbrella of the interdisciplinary Open Phonetics Working Gathering (OWLG), be that as it may, such a cooperation might be conceivable, on the grounds that it addresses one of the not very many gatherings where the two networks really meet. The Etymological Connected Open Information Cloud Late years have seen not just various ways to deal with give phonetic information as Connected Information, yet additionally the development of bigger drives that target interconnecting these assets.

Among these, the Open Etymology Working Gathering (OWLG) of the Open Information Establishment (OKFN) has led the production of new information and the republishing of existing etymological assets as a feature of the arising Phonetic Connected Open Information (LLOD) cloud. These drives give innovative framework and local area support for specialists wishing to create and share under-resourced language information.

The LLOD Cloud Beside benefits emerging from the genuine connecting of etymological assets, different semantic assets from altogether different fields have been given in RDF and related norms throughout the past 10 years. Specifically, this is the situation for lexical assets like WordNet (Gangemi, Navigli, and Velardi 2003), which addresses a foundation of the Semantic Web and is solidly coordinated in the Connected Open Information (LOD) cloud. From a more extensive perspective, LOD general information bases from the LOD, for example, the DBpedia have likewise been delivered as lexical assets, attributable to their characteristic significance for Normal Language Handling undertakings like Named Substance Acknowledgment (NER) or Anaphora Goal (AR).

Different kinds of phonetically applicable assets with less significance to simulated intelligence and information portrayal, in any case, are not a customary piece of the LOD cloud, in spite of the fact that they do spur the formation of a sub-cloud devoted to etymological assets. Figure 4.8 represents the Semantic Connected Open Information (LLOD) cloud outline. The LLOD cloud is an assortment of phonetic assets that are distributed (normally) under open licenses as Connected Information. The information are decentralized, created, and kept up with metadata online.

The cloud graph is created as a local area exertion with regards to OWLG and is constructed consequently from metadata about Connected Information sources put away on the web. Clients who wish to have their datasets included need to ensure that something like one URL accommodated information or endpoints is ready. Metadata labels for discoverability incorporate model (Forkel 2014).

The Open Semantics Working Gathering The LLOD cloud is a consequence of an organized exertion by the Open Etymology Working Bunch (OWLG; see Chiarcos and Pareja-Lora, this volume). Since its development in 2010, the OWLG has developed consistently. One of our essential objectives is to achieve transparency in etymology through:

1. Advancing open phonetic assets

2. Fostering the means for the portrayal of Open Information

3. Empowering the trading of thoughts across various disciplines Distributing phonetic information under open licenses is a significant issue in scholastic examination, as well as in the advancement of utilizations.

We see expanding support for this in the semantics local area (Pederson 2008), and there are a developing number of assets distributed under open licenses (Meyers et al. 2007). Distributing assets under open licenses offers many benefits: For example, unreservedly accessible information can be all the more handily reused, twofold ventures can be kept away from, and results can be imitated. Likewise, different scientists can expand on the information and consequently can allude to the distributions related with them. By and by, various moral, lawful, and humanistic issues are related with Open Data,45 and the advancements that lay out interoperability (and in this way reusability) of phonetic assets are still a work in progress. The OWLG addresses an open discussion for intrigued people to address these and related issues.

At the hour of composing, the gathering comprises of around 100 individuals from 20 distinct nations. Our gathering is somewhat little, however constantly developing and adequately heterogeneous. It incorporates individuals from library science, typology, verifiable phonetics, mental science, computational etymology, and data innovation; the ground for productive interdisciplinary conversations has been spread out. One substantial outcome arising out of joint efforts between an enormous number of OWLG individuals is the LLOD cloud, as currently outlined previously. Free examination exercises of numerous local area individuals include the utilization of RDF/OWL to address phonetic corpora, lexical-semantic assets, wording archives, and metadata assortments about semantic information assortments and distributions.

To numerous such individuals, the Connected Open Information worldview addresses an especially engaging arrangement of innovations. Inside the OWLG, these exercises have united toward building the cloud. Under-Resourced Dialects in the LLOD Cloud Two chief main impetuses of the development of the LLOD cloud chart and the OWLG have been, first, the collaborations between autonomous exploration projects whose specialists were keen on giving their information as RDF or Open Information, and, second, global tasks, frequently financed by the EU, that emphasis on innovative answers for multilinguality issues in the European computerized single market (influencing matters of confinement, computational etymology, and machine interpretation).

A third variable that added to this improvement has been later undertakings and applications in the humanities and scholastic parts of semantics. With the exploration depicted in this paper, we exhibit the appropriateness of LLOD advancements to one of these "little" areas of examination and their capacity to saddle their exceptionally unambiguous assets in concentrating under-resourced dialects. We consider the transformation of this innovation in a space where the two specialists and understudies are many times lacking programming abilities to be an especially impressive case for the capability of Connected Information in phonetics.

Notwithstanding, the QuantHistLing projects and CLLD are just two commendable contextual investigations from this specific region. Related endeavors that utilize RDF as well as Semantic Connected Open Information for the review and correlation of less-resourced dialects incorporate, for instance, the "Typology Apparatus" TYTO (Schalley 2012) that uses Semantic Web advances to process, coordinate, and inquiry cross-etymological information. The Typological Data set System46 (Dimitriadis et al. 2009) involves OWL ontologies for orchestrating and giving admittance to appropriated data sets that are made over typological exploration and language documentation.

For a comparable application in language asset harmonization, the GOLD philosophy was made as a component of the Electronic Metastructure for Jeopardized Dialects Information (E-Merge, see Langendoen, this volume). Poornima and Great (2010) have previously portrayed the utilization of RDF and Connected Information advances for making machine-meaningful wordlists for under-resourced dialects. Expanding on these and different bits of prior research, the task called Connected Open Word references (LiODi) is at present creating methods to work with cross-etymological inquiry across word references to aid language contact studies among jeopardized and authentic dialects in the Caucasus region and among Turkic dialects (Abromeit et al. 2016), as well as to aid the LLOD change of configurations commonly utilized in etymological typology furthermore, for language documentation (Chiarcos et al. 2017).

While these advances and the assets made on this premise are still being worked on, the PanLex project (Kamholz, Pool, and Colowick 2014) has previously distributed a close widespread RDF-based interpretation chart that covers various under-resourced dialects. Getting Extra Direction Similar to the situation when specialists embrace any best in class innovations, advances and improvements are occurring quicker than customary print media might perhaps stay aware of.

In this paper, we gave sound thinking and instances of why we accept Connected Information is a significant stage for working with and scattering under-resourced language information. By the by, the instruments and advancements right now up to speed will have definitely acquired a lot of ground before this volume comes to press. Accordingly, we have assembled a vault where we store our new instructive materials and DIY instructional exercises for clients who wish to execute and distribute models of Etymological Connected Open Information with their own assets. This section gives an overall prologue to Connected Information and its application in the language sciences, with a particular accentuation on its purposes for concentrating under-resourced dialects.

We distinguished qualities of information for such dialects, zeroing in on lexical assets (wordlists and word references) and on clarified corpora (shines and corpora). We further examined parts of asset incorporation, prior to zeroing in on Connected Information and under-resourced language information specifically. We then, at that point, homed in on Connected Information for phonetics and NLP, and we gave two brief contextual analyses of semantic information sources that have been changed into Connected Information. At last, we portrayed exhaustively the status and the transfer speed of uses of Connected Open Information advances to under-resourced dialects in the overall setting of the Open Etymology Working Gathering and the creating Phonetic Connected Open Information (LLOD) biological system.

5. A Data Category Repository for Language Resources

DatCatInfo is an internet based asset of data about information classifications (DCs) that are utilized in normal language handling applications and in the innovative work of language assets. The assortment was initially called "the Information Class Vault" and regularly referred to as the "DCR." Kept up with under the web address https://www .isocat.org, this assortment was created by the Global Association for Normalization Specialized Board 37 for Language and Wording (ISO/TC 37) and was arranged as a normalized ISO Library, with the Maximum Planck Establishment for Psycholinguistics (Nijmegen, the Netherlands; hereinafter assigned as MPI) going about as an authority Enlistment Authority. Over the long haul obviously albeit many language specialists were keen on recording information classifications, scarcely any upheld normalizing them by following a three-stage balloting method recommended by ISO.

Thusly, the "Vault" has been rechristened a "Information Classification Vault," and it has been going through a significant refit starting around 2014. In this article and different distributions about DatCatInfo and its set of experiences, the expression "Library" is accordingly saved for the ISO supported asset (up to 2014), and "Vault" is utilized for DatCatInfo (after 2014). The deep rooted abbreviation "DCR," once utilized for "Information Classification Vault" in settings portraying "DatCatInfo," presently alludes to "Information Class Archive." The primary motivation behind DatCatInfo is to help the advancement of language assets, but DatCatInfo is itself a language asset. This section will consequently begin with a brief conversation about language assets. As per the European Language Asset Affiliation (ELRA), the term language asset alludes to "a bunch of discourse or language information and depictions in machine decipherable structure," like electronic corpora, wording information bases (termbases), and computational vocabularies (ELRA 2017).

These assets are used to help a large number of utilizations that are vital for the computerized economy, for example, discourse acknowledgment and amalgamation, information mining, website streamlining, content examination and the executives, centered promoting, machine interpretation, and the language administrations industry overall (interpretation, deciphering, and confinement). Language assets are unavoidable: They are a center part of PC working frameworks, they are fundamental for efficiency applications like office suites (word handling, calculation sheets, and such), they are utilized in numerous sorts of robotized modern and business hardware, and they are even found in phones. At the point when we make an internet based buy, utilize a mechanized telephone utility, or send an instant message, we are utilizing language assets.

Supposed man-made reasoning (computer based intelligence) applications are underlying part on broad language assets. Language assets are made and overseen by interpreters, terminologists, word specialists, etymologists, analysts, computer programmers, and various different experts, numerous utilizing specific computational programming. They are created in scholastic examination settings, in business conditions, and in open foundations too. First created on paper, and refined over the long haul in computerized conditions, language assets have developed in lined up with language industry norms.

For example, text corpora have become all the more impressive and valuable as language assets with the advancement of the explanation system guidelines delivered in ISO/TC 37, and termbases depend on models portrayed in hypothetical principles like ISO 704, as well as in useful norms for example, ISO 30042, the TermBase Trade standard (TBX). Without norms, creating language assets would be considerably more costly than needed, many advances and undertakings would should be copied that could somehow be completed just a single time, and it would be difficult to use data across language assets and across various applications. To put it plainly, inadequate with regards to principles, our general public wouldn't have the scope of language assets, and the applications that are empowered by them, that we have today.

Information Classifications One of the critical areas of normalization that applies to language assets connects with their inward information structures — what sorts of information they contain and how these information are organized. For instance, before a spell checker can decide if a word is accurately spelled or not, it requirements to "know" in the event that the word is a thing, action word, descriptor, or other grammatical feature. "I prompt [verb] my companion, however I offer my companion guidance [noun]."

The distinction — s or c — relies upon the grammatical feature. Grammatical feature data is likewise pivotal for semantic-based assets, like electronic word references and ontologies — since, notwithstanding the closeness in importance, the meaning of the action word won't be indistinguishable from that of the thing. How words are arranged by their grammatical form can be normalized, making spell checkers, as well as the numerous other language assets that utilization grammatical form data, more interoperable. The grammatical feature is an illustration of a semantic information class (DC). There are hundreds, in the event that not thousands, of various DCs that are tracked down in language assets or are utilized to portray and oversee ideas, names, information designs, and methodology normal to language assets.

There are likewise various sorts of DCs and an extensive variety of conceivable ways of reporting and depict them.In the 1990s, language specialists and scientists, however specifically terminologists who were planning phrasing the board frameworks, started to share information about DCs, with a point to orchestrate approaches and techniques. In this setting Wright and Budin led a review that recorded DCs in all the then-accessible phrasing the executives frameworks — which were army at that point, yet the greater part of which are presently old, as well as some public term banks, including Termium, Danterm, and, surprisingly, the old Sovterm (Wright and Budin 1994). At last, ISO TC 37, then, at that point, accused essentially of creating guidelines for the area of phrasing the executives, started harmonization endeavors, which thusly drove the ISO TC in 1999 to distribute determinations for 215 DCs in the norm: ISO 12620 — PC applications in phrasing — Information classes. As it were, this standard contained the first launch of DatCatInfo. ISO 12620:1999 presented the term information class determination, which is the amount of data that portrays a DC.

The design and content of an information classification detail as reported in that standard is displayed in figure 5.1. The DCs in 12620:1999 were gathered specifically, as displayed in the list of chapters (figure 5.2). This topical association, specifically the division among idea and term, generally mirrors the primary levels of an expressed passage as determined in ISO 12200, MachineReadable Phrasing Exchange Organization (MARTIF), an underlying model that in 2003 was normalized in ISO 16642-Phrased Markup Structure (TMF). The markup for termbases depicted in ISO 12200 was serialized in Standard Summed up Markup Language (ISO 8879:1986), which later brought about XML. ISO 12200 additionally lines up with the purported meta-components (, , and) in TBX, the XML markup language for phrasing (supplanting the SGML of ISO 12200), which in 2008 was distributed as ISO 30042. Consequently, the elaboration of information classifications has continued in lined up with the advancement of different assets (like the Internet) and other principles that are natural today. A few DCs accept free text as their substance, for example,/definition/(Proviso A.5.1 in ISO 12620),1 while the substance of others is bound to a shut arrangement of reasonable qualities, for example,/syntactic orientation/(A.2.2.2), which can contain just the qualities manly, ladylike, fix, or other. The kind of satisfied that a DC can take is alluded to as its substance model. ISO 12620:1999 didn't plainly recognize DCs as indicated by their substance models. A portion of the reasonable qualities were treated as DCs themselves with full information class particulars (for example, the 19 upsides of/term type/in Conditions A.2.1.1-A.2.1.19), while others were only recorded in the information class detail of their "parent" DC — for example, the previously mentioned upsides of/syntactic orientation/are recorded as (a), (b), (c), and (d) in A.2.2.2. Notwithstanding, around then, ISO 12620 was disseminated in paper design just, so this engaging approach, albeit incidentally conflicting, didn't cause serious application issues.

ISO 12620:1999 likewise presented the idea of an information classification choice (DCS). Since no termbase would contain every one of the 215 DCs, it was perceived that terminologists would select those DCs that were essential for the reason and clients of their termbases. Various choices of DCs would be expected for various kinds of termbases, as, for example, an administration supported term bank recording a country's true dialects versus a corporate termbase intended to help worldwide advertising. Whatever choices could become perceived as a best practice for specific applications and purposes. Every determination of DCs was alluded to as a DCS. ISO 12620:1999 denoted a significant achievement in the improvement of phrasing assets what's more, of wording the executives as a training. It empowered terminologists to start orchestrating their termbases, along these lines delivering them more interoperable and repurposable, and, as recently referenced, it likewise went about as an impetus for the improvement of different norms. The idea of harmonization suggests the utilization of uniform DC names and industry settlement on DC definitions or portrayals, two elements that are fundamental to trade information among various termbases. Proposition for an Information Class Vault At the point when ISO 12620:1999 was expected for methodical audit five years after the fact, ISO TC 37 chose that a significant change was essential.

At around a similar time, the sub-panel TC 37/SC 4, "Language Asset The executives," was made, getting partners fields of language asset the board past phrasing, (for example, lexicology, morphology, explanation plans, and corpus the executives) into the TC 37 local area, alongside the new kinds of language assets that these partners create. The first number of DCs — 215 — expected to build essentially to oblige their necessities. Moreover, circulating data about DCs in a paper record that was refreshed just a single time like clockwork, best case scenario, and that sold for more than $300 USD, was not OK to most of clients, who undeniably required DCs as open information that could be joined, subsetted, and controlled in different applications. DC details required to be treated as discrete units of data — smaller than normal reports themselves that are more helpful for impromptu query and liable to visit increases and updates — like things in a web-based list.

It was accordingly suggested that an electronic variant of the information classification details be made as an internet based data set. Moving information class particulars from paper to electronic organization was built up by the far reaching want to make a cooperative, online climate where designers and scientists in semantics and related disciplines could archive the kinds of information that they work with, which at last would increment interoperability, diminish duplication and overt repetitiveness, and cultivate research also, development. As would be found later, be that as it may, this sort of climate, where the etymological local area in general would be partaking on a regular premise, proved unable rigorously stick to the proper normalization model directed by ISO. The vital differentiation to be made here is normalization versus harmonization: settlement on names and content without formal balloting for every single information classification particular.

While ISO/TC 37 was planning its electronic asset for information classification determinations, ISO Focal Secretariat (CS) was arranging a comparative drive for different guidelines, which it named the Idea Information base (ISO/CDB). The CDB would have permitted web-based query of various information objects found in distributed ISO norms, including terms and definitions, graphical images, codes (language, country, money, and so on), units of estimation, item properties, and things in information word references. Albeit a pilot form was sent off in 2009, the task was displaced by the right now accessible ISO Internet Perusing Stage (ISO 2018; Kemps-Snijders et al. 2009).

In the shadow of CDB advancement, the future TC 37 DC data set was to be known as the Information Classification Library (DCR), since it was imagined that information classification particulars would, as verified previously, turn into "normalized" and "enrolled" under ISO's Enlistment Authority (RA) model. To make the DCR, it was important to initially characterize the information model and administration methodology. Over a time of quite a long while, ISO/TC 37 explained the vital system, distributed as ISO 12620:2009 — Determination of information classifications and the executives of a Information Class Library for language assets. It means quite a bit to take note of that this variant of 12620 contains no real DC determinations. Rather, it frames the information model and the system for making and dealing with the future DCR. 12620:2009 was expounded in close coordinated effort with agents from ISO Focal Secretariat, to guarantee that the DCR would uphold the normalization of DCs in understanding with the CDB. As recently noticed, the Maximum Planck Establishment for Psycholinguistics (MPI) was delegated by the ISO Specialized Administration Board to be the Enlistment Authority. 12620:2009 covered the accompanying subjects, among others:

Since DC details were currently given in electronic structure just, their construction required to have been very thorough, and the reliable announcement of DC values became fundamental. It was chosen to think about the worth of a DC, for example,/ladylike/for/syntactic orientation/, to be an information classification by its own doing and to be named a straightforward DC. All different DCs are considered to be intricate in light of the fact that, dissimilar to basic DCs, they have a calculated space, or at least, a "set of substantial worth implications" (12620:2009, Proviso 3.1.5).

Legitimate worth implications are either (a) extremely open in nature, for example, for the DC/definition/, which can contain free text, or (b) obliged by a standard, for example, for/date/, which follows a specific configuration, or on the other hand (c) rigorously obliged to just a shut arrangement of listed (reasonable) values, that is to say, communicated by straightforward DCs, like the qualities/thing/,/action word/,/modifier/for the shut DC /grammatical feature/.

The accompanying typology of DCs in view of their substance model was expounded. In this typology, the calculated space is a key separating factor: • Complex DC: DC that has a theoretical space ◦ Open DC: complex DC whose calculated space isn't confined to an identified set of values, for example, a/definition/ ◦ Obliged DC: complex DC whose applied space is non-counted, yet is confined to a requirement determined in a composition explicit language or dialects, such as a/date/or a scope of dates ◦ Shut DC: complex DC whose theoretical space is limited to a bunch of specified straightforward information classes, for example,/grammatical feature/ • Basic DC: DC that doesn't have a reasonable space, yet is itself an individual from a one, for example,/thing/, or/action word/for/grammatical feature/ Separating DCs in view of the reasonable area would direct the plan of the information model representing things to come DCR.An Elaborate Information Model To oblige both the new advanced design and the normalization and enrollment work processes, the information classification determination model in 12620:2009 should have been more thorough contrasted with its 1999 ancestor.

Every DC particular contained various settled segments, every one of which incorporated numerous fields for metadata:

• Administration Information Section • Description Section ○ Data Element Name Section ○ Language Section ◘ Name Section ◘ Definition Section ◘ Example Section ◘ Explanation Section • Conceptual Domain • Linguistic Section ○ Conceptual Domain ○ Example Section

The Maximum Planck Foundation (MPI) acted not just as the DCR's Enrollment Authority (RA); it likewise took on a much bigger job in specialized advancement, upkeep, facilitating, and indeed, even advancement, under the heading of the DCR Board. The board included individuals from ISO/TC 37/SC 3, led by Dr. Sue Ellen Wright, a co-creator of this part. MPI offered these types of assistance from send off in 2008 for the rest of 2014. Specialists related with the MPI started populating the DCR with information classification determinations.

The information classification assortment that had been collected in TC 37 and during various past exploration endeavors (eminently the SALT undertaking, DXLT Particular, 2000) and that had upheld the first ISO 12620, was brought into the new ISOcat climate pretty much flawless, with more prominent consideration paid to the assortment of extra information than to the refinement of existing assets. Under the protection of the CLARIN project (CLARIN 2017; see Trippel and Zinn, this volume) scientists keen on characterizing ideas utilized in information mining and data recovery across connected semantic assets started to archive DCs that reflected interests going from fundamental semantic and syntactic investigation to profoundly specific assortments, for example, another Clean public termbase. Expansive profiles (a kind of semantic order utilized in the DCR) that apply to an extensive variety of different language assets, like Morphosyntax and Metadata, developed in the DCR in lined up with the verifiable space explicit profiles of Wording and Etymology.

More unambiguous profiles, like Gesture based communication, additionally came to fruition. The DCR bit by bit welcomed members from different phonetic networks to share their information, which came about in the expansion of, for example, the GOLD philosophy classifications (see Langendoen, this volume) and other comparative assortments into the DCR. Subsequently, during those initial six years, the DCR experienced great development. Beginning with the 215 DCs from 12620:1999, it developed to incorporate an impressive 6,185 DCs from a dozen etymological disciplines. In excess of 150 specialists from almost 80 associations contributed. To a great extent because of this cooperative methodology, the ISO-propelled normalization work process that had been integrated into the plan was rarely utilized.

One work to test that work process was a horrid disappointment. With no committed staff to go about as guardians of the DCR, quality couldn't be guaranteed, and duplication, overt repetitiveness, and different issues started to happen. A portion of the topical region of the DCR were legitimate, while others were ignored, bringing about lopsidedness. The DCR experienced becoming excessively quick without committed assets. Moreover, much of the time the power applied to the undertaking was not generally met with equivalent meticulousness, bringing about impressive contrasts in quality among the passages. The first TC 37 arrangement of DCs had been explained via prepared terminologists, who tended to keep severe guidelines for composing definitions and cautious systems for explaining information class details.

A few arrangements of DCs were initially expounded in different dialects and afterward interpreted (not generally well) into the base language, which was English, while different sections were converted into various dialects, with changing levels of achievement. The arising assortment showed critical irregularities in quality and expectation, essentially as the consequence of a semi cloud-obtaining climate that, to some extent, needed firm administration. Withdrawal of the Maximum Planck Organization and Determination of Termweb The first reason of the DCR was that DCs are fixed; for example, a thing is a thing, no matter where it happens in a language asset. Over the long run it turned out to be clear, in any case, that various networks of training expected to involve DCs in various ways. Albeit genuine termbase advancement is frequently chaotic and often neglects to stick to ideal practice, terminologists planning the first DCR needed to involve DCs as obviously characterized field names in their termbases in a manner that would uphold solid information exchange.

Specifically, the cautious particular of applied space data was basic for fashioners who believed their information should adjust to a trade model. Conversely, clients related with MPI started to understand that they required a store comprised of phonetic ideas utilized fairly like thesaurus marks for adaptable information recovery instead of one containing officially characterized DCs with thoroughly controlled reasonable areas. There is, as a matter of fact, a significant differentiation to be made between a semantic idea and an etymological DC, a qualification that was not, yet has not been, expressly expressed. The information model of the DCR was not great for archiving such ideas; it contained metadata and designs expected to depict DCs, yet not required, or even counterproductive, for portraying etymological ideas, and MPI clients in this manner thought that it is pointlessly complicated.

This, combined with a change in asset designations at MPI, drove MPI to choose to pull out from the DCR toward the finish of 2014. While at first vexing to TC 37, MPI's choice prompted an chance to audit the ongoing framework and functional system with a point toward further developing convenience, quality, and trustworthiness. Subsequent to assessing potential substitution frameworks, TC 37 chose TermWeb, which is a wording the executives framework presented by Interverbum Innovation. TermWeb is completely versatile for overseeing discrete units of content of different sorts, not simply phrasing, furthermore, it ended up being a reasonable application for lodging the substance of the DCR. The essential local area to be served by the DCR in its new setup remains terminologists planning termbase models, especially those functioning with regards to ISO 30042, as well as ISO 12616 for Interpretation situated terminography.

The new DCR is facilitated on a TermWeb information base case. A reciprocal site, datcatinfo.net, goes about as a door to the TermWeb asset and gives data about the undertaking. It is intently facilitated with tbxinfo.org, an electronic summary of particulars and utilities intended to work with the creation, control, and trade of phrased information, particularly in XLIFF-mindful conditions (ISO 21720). Execution of TBX tongues intended for effective and exact trade of termbase content is explicitly connected to the DCs kept in the DCR. A second local area that depends on the DCR is upheld by the Lexical Markup Structure (LMF) standard, ISO/WD 24613-5.

Tentative arrangements for fostering a planning instrument among TBX and LMF depend on the coordination of reasonable information classifications between the two guidelines. In December 2014, the progress started from the web application created by MPI to TermWeb. MPI exchanged the unique DCR it had created to static (read-just) mode furthermore, gave the DCR Board (which had now declined into a less-formal administration board) with duplicates of the static documents containing the information classification determinations. In equal, the CLARIN bunch has kept up with its Idea Library starting around 2015. Moving the DCR to TermWeb Moving the information class details to TermWeb was not clear. Since the assortment had developed under a publicly supporting model without intelligible substance the board, the principal task was to procure a profound comprehension of the information.

Given the worries over quality, it was vital for rank subsets of DC determinations as indicated by certainty level, as well as to recognize and eliminate the pieces of the information model that were either excess or then again presently excessive. The methodology embraced was to read up the diagram for the Information Classification Exchange Organization (DCIF), which was the occupant XML markup language for addressing information classification particulars inside ISOcat, in other words, in the first DCR. DCIF contained 43 components, 18 credits, and 43 information types — a sum of 104 distinct examples of markup strings. The DCR contained 6,185 DC determinations, every one being reported in a separate record named .dcif. For example,/grammatical feature/was 396.dcif. Factual investigation utilizing the Scholar Devices concordancer uncovered how the 104 DCIF strings were really utilized in the 6,185 dcif records. The upside of Scribe over other concordancers is that it permits clump look, which implied that each of the 104 DCIF strings could be submitted for investigation across every one of the 6,185 dcif records without a moment's delay.

(Other concordancers accessible at the time just permitted each string to be looked through in turn.) Scribe creates a cluster report that shows the recurrence of event of each string. It was accordingly discovered that six components, five ascribes, and practically every one of the information types — 20% of the all out markup curios — were missing or so uncommon in the dcif documents that they could be disposed of without loss of data. In the old DCR, the individual who initially made a DC was recorded as its "proprietor." At first, the DC was given a "private" scope esteem; the proprietor was the main individual who could get to it. At the point when the proprietor felt that the DC could hold any importance with a more extensive local area also, was open to sharing it, the person could change the extension to "public," which made it accessible to different clients. There were 1,954 confidential DCs and 4,231 public DCs in the set provided by MPI. Scribe results additionally uncovered continuous duplications, strange or sketchy substance, inaccurately utilized fields, and different issues. These issues happened less as often as possible in the public DCs contrasted with the confidential ones, the previous profiting from the checks furthermore, balances of the group.

Hence, the public DCs were relocated first. As expressed before, the Etymological Segment was planned to permit language-explicit models, clarifications, and reasonable spaces; it was expected to be a subset of the DC-level applied space. A habitually refered to instance of the requirement for language-explicit calculated spaces is the DC/syntactic orientation/(1297), where admissible qualities for French are /mama , though German additionally permits/fix/, as displayed in figure 5.3. In any case, the Semantic Segment had been the subject of negative client criticism: It comprised an extra settled level in the information model, added intricacy to the UI, what's more, had demonstrated hard for clients to accurately apply. It worked out that main 37 DCs contained an Etymological Segment, or around 0.6%. Moreover, generally speaking, it had been abused. For example, in nine DCs it was vacant. In 22 DCs there was just a single Phonetic Segment, and it either didn't give any extra data or it contained just a model, which could undoubtedly be moved to the higher language Area.

Just six public DCs (under 0.2%) contained Etymological Segments that could be legitimate. The first aim of the Phonetic Area stays substantial, as it is now and again important to express something about a DC for a particular language. Be that as it may, making an unmistakable design in the information model for such a seldom happening highlight isn't legitimate. Such data can be kept in a Note or other field of the Language Segment. Killing the Etymological Area works on the information model significantly, makes the new DCR (the Information Class Vault) simpler to utilize, and disposes of information overt repetitiveness. Another key finding connects with the applied areas themselves.

A few DCs have, or were imagined to have, different theoretical areas for various etymological applications. For instance, the passable upsides of a DC could be different for wording assets instead of one more kind of language asset, for example, morphological comment plans. In any case, again it was fascinating to consider whether the rate of various calculated spaces for various application regions was genuinely critical. Limiting DCs to one calculated space at a time would further improve on the new information model.

The investigation showed that main four public DCs (less than 0.1%) had mutiple substantial calculated area. This factual proof cast uncertainty on the requirement for permitting numerous reasonable spaces in a DC. For the interesting situations where application-explicit reasonable spaces are required, for example, the/grammatical feature/, which requires many qualities for Morphosyntax yet a couple for different applications, making separate DCs for each case would

be a sensible arrangement. It very well may be contended that when the passable upsides of a DC wander impressively in various semantic applications, what we are truly managing is unique information class ideas. This was, for sure, the viewpoint previously taken by clients of the DCR; it contained seven unique DCs covering the idea of/grammatical feature/. Refusing numerous application-explicit theoretical spaces for a DC was in this manner chose. Figures 5.4 and 5.5 show two DC details for/grammatical feature/from TermWeb.

Figure 5.4 is the DC arranged for Morphosyntax, and figure 5.5 is the DC applied to Wording. Note the distinctions in the applied space, displayed as Relations in TermWeb. The applied space of/grammatical feature/for Morphosyntax contains some more individuals than that for Wording. Figure 5.6 shows the individuals from the calculated space for Wording in a graph design. With the investment of a worldwide local area of partners, the DCR had turned into a publicly supported asset, working for all functional purposes outside the formal ISO climate. The work processes that were created to allow normalization of DCs as indicated by the conventional ISO stages were rarely utilized. Without a doubt, during six years of activity, not a solitary DC detail was normalized in the DCR.

This reality couldn't be disregarded what's more, drove the administration panel to perceive that the DCR served a harmonization, instead of a normalization, job. Hence, the normalization work process areas of the DCIF model, which included significant pieces of the Organization Segment, were disposed of.

The DCR upholds recording DC details in 37 dialects, and more can be added. Be that as it may, presently, there is no satisfied for 11 dialects, and very little for a small bunch of others. Simultaneously, questions have been raised about the requirement for any dialects other than English. For sure, the order of the DCR is to portray DCs, not to "decipher" them. Then again, the TermWeb framework upholds multilingual substance out-of-the-case, so the multilingual idea of the asset has been kept up with, even however doing so implied that it is important to survey and keep up with the multilingual data close by the English substance. To sum up, the Phonetic Area and the pieces of the Authoritative Segment that upheld the ISO normalization work process have been disposed of, and the Calculated Area has been confined to just a single example for every DC.

Figure 5.7 shows the first information model with the eliminated parts crossed out. Changing DCIF over completely to TBX As expressed before, the source documents from the DCR were serialized in a particular organization called DCIF. TermWeb just backings import of XML records that are in TermBase Trade (TBX) design. Thusly, the DCIF documents should have been changed over completely to TBX, which is adequately granular to address the DCIF parts that were held after examination and correction. In any case, DCIF addresses information classifications, while TBX addresses wording. Albeit the design of the two information models was comparative, there were adequate contrasts to make the change very testing. To begin with, the DCIF components and qualities were planned to identical TBX structures. This involved not simply changing the name of a component or a trait, however in some cases likewise moving a component to an alternate area in the section model, or changing over data from an component name to a quality worth or from a trait worth to component content.

In June 2016, Kara Warburton, a co-creator of this part, arranged a determination report framing the planning prerequisites. LTAC Worldwide, a not-for-profit consortium that upholds drives advancing interoperability of language assets, liberally offered the types of assistance of a computer programmer who fostered a transformation script in light of the determination. The accompanying guidelines were executed in the content. a) Eliminate undesirable DCIF markup Markup addressing data that would become repetitive or superfluous in the objective framework, for example, verifiable dates, client names, and settling components that don't have TBX partners, should have been taken out. Moreover, the individuals from the calculated space of a shut DC, (for example,/thing/for /grammatical feature/) couldn't be straightforwardly brought into TermWeb. The singular basic DCs themselves (/thing/, and so forth) were imported consequently by the movement script, yet entirely their participation in the parent shut DC couldn't be addressed in the import document. This is on the grounds that the connection between a straightforward DC and its parent is laid out in TermWeb by means of a "connection," and relations are not importable.

Those components were in this way additionally eliminated from the parent DC details in the import record. After import, the relations were laid out physically by language specialists working in TermWeb. Table 5.1 gives instances of markup eliminated from the first DCIF.

The following stage was to audit every one of the nine records before import physically. During this survey, a couple of issues in the transformation cycle were found and answered to the product engineer, who refreshed the change script, and the transformation was then rehashed. These issues were much of the time credited to absent or erroneous data in the movement determination, normally on the grounds that the full scope of data types and occasions in huge number of dcif documents couldn't be expected. The survey made it conceivable to recognize and resolve many substance related issues previously bringing the DC determinations into TermWeb. The progressions that were made incorporate the following: • Taking out overt repetitiveness: For example, a similar bibliographical reference was frequently refered to over and over in a similar DC, and at times various fields contained copy data (like Legitimization and Definition). Moving data to the ideal locations:

For example, on the off chance that a Definition was really an Clarification or a Note, it was moved in like manner. • Parting consolidated data to isolate fields: For example, when a Definition field included both a definition and a note, the note part was moved as needs be. • Settling boundless or mysterious documentations: For example, abbreviations utilized for individuals' names and truncated types of different sorts. Possibly new contractions, like

T9n/L10n, were extended to their legitimate formulations.• Eliminating old or insignificant documentations, for example, "green text," which was a verifiable documentation at this point not pertinent. • Fixing typographical blunders and spelling botches. • Fixing organizing issues.

Eliminating components that contained just placeholder text. • Eliminating Beginning qualities that are excessively broad, for example "etymology writing." • Really taking a look at URLs and eliminating or supplanting broken joins. • Fixing various mistaken DC names. Other more-considerable changes were suggested, however it was felt that meaningful changes ought to be talked about with agent partners ahead of time. For this reason, a field called "Commentator remarks" was made in TermWeb, alongside a comparing component in the TBX import record. A sum of 385 commentator remarks were incorporated in the import record. Anybody working in DatCatInfo can utilize this field to record ideas. To save a duplicate of the first information, should any of the progressions be addressed in the future, by and large XML remarking labels were embedded around the first satisfied furthermore, the new rectified variant was added close by the first.

There are presently 4,984 sets of remarking labels. Taking into account the quantity of analyst remarks and XML remarking labels, almost 5,400 alters, changes, and ideas were made to the imported DC details. While more work is as yet required, huge headway has proactively been made in tending to past worries about quality. Another issue was copy passages. Copies During the survey, a critical number of copy DCs, or DCs that are possibly copy, were found.

Different text investigation devices were utilized to gauge the extent of duplication, in light of contrasting the DC names. Five percent (160) of the imported DCs have a similar name as another DC. These DCs should be checked to decide which are real copies, and their DC details fit. For the DCs not yet imported, the potential duplication is bigger: 10% (335). It will be important to address those copies before import.

These figures address DCs whose names are indistinguishable. Be that as it may, copy DC details additionally happen where the names are not indistinguishable. A few deal signs in light of similitudes in the DC name — for example,/legal deciphering/,/legal executive translation/, and/legal executive deciphering/. Others have no likenesses in the names at all, yet assessment of other metadata can affirm that as a matter of fact they allude to a similar DC idea. This issue addresses a significant part representing things to come harmonization exercises: The whole DCR needs to be assessed to distinguish and determine copies. Beside copies, there are likewise situations where the DC's status as a DC was problematic. What Is an Information Class, and What Isn't? For some DC determinations, questions were raised whether what was being portrayed was a information class. The primary gathering of problematic DC determinations includes the "etymological ideas" entered to address issues in the CLARIN project.

A semantic idea isn't really likewise an occurrence of genuine information in any language asset. For example, DC 3998 is /language for unique purposes/(LSP). The DC definition was taken from ISO 1087, which is a glossary, and is now freely accessible in the ISO OBP. Is "language for extraordinary purposes" likewise an information classification utilized in some language asset? Conceivably. The risk is in tolerating without question phonetic ideas into the DCR. An unmistakable differentiation should be made between semantic ideas and etymological information classes, with unadulterated ideas most likely being confined in a document. The second gathering of sketchy DC particulars incorporates code strings, for example, the name of a component or a characteristic from a XML jargon or explanation conspire. Numerous of this kind started from the Text Encoding Drive (TEI). For instance, DC 6186, basically called/a/, is from the TEI header. Another model is DC 2794,/ADJA/, which is depicted as the "STTS tag for attributive descriptor."

Yet the DCR as of now has two DCs called/attributive descriptive word/(1243 and 5242). In all likelihood, then,/ADJA/is just a code portrayal of one of these current DCs, where it ought to be added as an elective DC name. How code portrayals ought to be dealt with should be chosen. The third gathering covers DCs from nonlinguistic areas, like clinical/logical ideas. For instance, DC 4458 depicts/magnetoencephalography/, and incorporates a portrayal from Wikipedia. Should the DCR try and incorporate such data? These DCs likely address information focuses utilized in reporting language-related physiological testing, however they aren't ordinarily connected with language assets fundamentally. DCs from outer sources, like Edisyn (2011), the GOLD philosophy (2010), and STTS (1995/1999), are as of now archived and kept up with by their source associations. The decision about whether to incorporate DCs that are as of now archived in another public asset is another far from being obviously true inquiry.

From one perspective, doing so addresses a type of duplication what's more, overt repetitiveness, and guaranteeing that the DC specification would be practically inconceivable is dependably cutting-edge and synchronized with its source rendition. Then again, one reason for the DCR is to offer a confided in wellspring of data about DCs in one helpful area. Having data about DCs in a single area cultivates harmonization. Dismissing all DCs that are reported in a current public asset would run opposite to the targets of the DCR. An authority choice in such manner has not been made. In themeantime, the DCs from these three associations have been briefly barred. One practical arrangement is keep a cross-reference section in the DCR that would point clients to other similar idea, term, or mark libraries.

Similarly as with any information base, there ought to be clear models for what meets all requirements for consideration. Sadly, there have all the earmarks of being no reported incorporation measures for the DCR. The new ISO 30042 and 12620 proposition a definition for information classification (ISO 30042, 3.8): information classification class of information things that are firmly related from a formal or semantic perspective Model:/grammatical form/,/subject field/,/definition/ Note 1 to passage: An information classification can be seen as a speculation of the idea of a field in a data set. By the by, the scope of content depicted in the DC determinations that were audited before relocation proposes that the numerous supporters of the assortment were working with no agreement of what an information class really is.

Without any unmistakable rules, generally speaking the problematic DC was kept in the import document and a commentator remark was incorporated to cause to notice the issue. Kinds of DCs that were eliminated from the import documents, and saved in a chronicle for future thought, are displayed in table 5.5

Post-Import Work As currently depicted, the principal significant undertaking after import was to lay out the connections between DCs with shut reasonable spaces and basic DCs that are the upsides of those areas. For example, it was important to connect/grammatical form/(DC 396) with/thing/(DC 1639),/action word/ (DC 1691). Other forthcoming undertakings incorporate tending to all the analyst remarks and choosing whether to ultimately import the DCs that were kept down in a file during this underlying import.

There is likewise the topic of continuous support, extra cleaning, checking, harmonization of copies, and expansion of new DCs. A Moving Character and Reason During the relocation among 2014 and late 2016, the council in control worked as an augmentation of ISO/TC 37/SC 3/WG 1 (Information Classes), and its standard advancement reports were introduced at the ISO/TC 37 yearly gatherings. It became obvious that the first reason and command of the DCR, as characterized in ISO 12620:2009, had changed, or required to change, since the normalization mission was rarely satisfied or even wanted.

Probably, clients required a confided in wellspring of data about DCs.

This can be accomplished through a less-formal course of union, audit, and harmonization. Besides, the DCR had endured "tasks getting out of control" in the application regions, which are alluded to as topical areas, that is to say, the disciplines covered inside the general class of semantics. ISO 12620:2009 expressed that the DCR is "relevant to a wide range of language assets" without offering a meaning of what qualifies as a language asset for this reason. Notwithstanding, in a few different spots in the norm, it is expressed that the purpose of the DCR was to cover information classes expected for ISO/TC 37 guidelines alone, as the accompanying citations illustrate: It will give a reference store to information classes and related data for all the current or on the other hand future guidelines in ISO/TC 37 that include information displaying or information trade (Proviso 5).

The production of a solitary worldwide Information Class Vault (DCR) for a wide range of language assets treated inside the ISO/TC 37 climate gives a bound together perspective on the different uses of such a reference asset (Presentation). The DCR will ultimately contain all ISO/TC 37 information classifications.... (Presentation). Likewise in the Presentation, four topical areas "have been perceived as quantifiable subsets of the DCR": Wording, Semantic Substance Portrayal, Language Codes, and Etymology. However Language Codes are now kept up with and made freely accessible by the US Library of Congress (LoC, 2013) and Ethnologue (2015). The connected Country Codes are accessible through the ISO

Web based Perusing Stage (ISO 2018). Two topical areas not referenced in ISO 12620:2009 became excessively huge in the DCR,

while the four unequivocally referenced remained underdocumented. The topical area most often utilized was "Uncertain." Other DC determinations, as currently referenced, portrayed ideas that are not piece of any phonetic space. Figure 5.8 shows the quantity of DCs that were allocated to each topical space. The Presentation in ISO 12620:2009 additionally expresses that "it isn't the plan of this Worldwide Norm to characterize a philosophy of language assets." by and large, this was an appalling oversight, as a cosmology of language assets would have worked on the utilization of the topical areas, which were intended to order DCs into intelligent subsets. (The justification behind this choice rested in a prior endeavor to arrange the DCs in ISO 12620:1999, a work that was broadly seen as a disappointment, basically on the grounds that the multi-layered nature of the DCs will in general block any mono-layered arrangement.)

Thus, in the DCR, the utilization of topical areas was conflicting, there was critical cross-over between the topical spaces themselves, the worth "Unsure" was broadly utilized, and DCs were much of the time relegated to different topical areas all the while. The last option is normal since DCs are much of the time utilized in different kinds of language assets. In any case, obviously the task of numerous topical spaces to a DC was not supported 100% of the time. The utilization of topical areas overall was exceptionally dangerous. Offered the shift from a conventional normalization job and the troubles related with the topical areas, the overseeing board chose to return to the command and extent of the DCR.

Formal normalization was deserted for less-formal harmonization and, considering the quality issues refered to above and the disarray over topical spaces, it was chosen to zero in promptly on the first topical area — Phrasing — to focus on the cleanup work. Hence, the DCs connecting with phrasing assets will be audited first in the new TermWeb climate. Rebranding: DatCatInfo The shift from normalization to harmonization as a reason implied that the new DCR was, basically, at this point not an ISO asset. Significant conversations about the consequences of these changes followed between the overseeing advisory group and ISO Focal Secretariat. It was commonly concurred that the DCR was not — and never had really been — an information class vault, yet rather had consistently filled the less-formal need of a vault. Therefore it was concurred that the abbreviation DCR would from now on address Information Class Vault. Since the DCR was not generally seen as an ISO asset, utilizing the current brand name ISOcat and the URL www.isocat.org was likewise not generally allowed.

The making due council closed a concurrence with ISO Focal Secretariat perceiving LTAC/TerminOrgs3 as the proprietor of the DCR. The name of the web space was changed to DatCatInfo and the URL to www.datcatinfo.net. By and by, a quest for www.isocat.org will divert to www.datcatinfo.net, and the DCR is firmly connected to www.tbxinfo.net, which gives data and utilities to the TBX standard. As a result of these changes,

ISO 12620:2009 was removed and another rendition has been created for distribution in 2019. It portrays best practices for fostering an Information Class Vault conventionally. As a result, the DCR itself is at this point not a standardizing asset claimed by ISO; rather, it is an assortment of industry-blended, industrysanctioned DCs. Model from DatCatInfo Figure 5.9 shows an information classification detail in DatCatInfo. The following are a couple of perceptions actually quite significant: • The Connection, showing that this DC has a nonexclusive connection facing up to DC 1948 (curtailed structure). This really intends that/truncation/is a straightforward DC and an individual from the applied space of/contracted structure/. The DC type straightforward can not set in stone by the Carried out as field, which demonstrates pick list esteem.

The Diligent Identifier (PID), which mirrors the document name (334) of the first DC particular from the previous Information Classification Vault. The isocat.org space name in the PIDs will ultimately be refreshed to datcatinfo.net. • The Identifier, "abbreviation." This is the machine-meaningful name of the DC. In compound names, the identifier is in this manner written in camel case, for example, partOfSpeech for /grammatical form/. • The Profile, "Wording," otherwise called the topical area. • The English name, "abbreviation," and the Information class name, "abbreviation" (red fields in the e-bar form). The last option is intended to be a language-skeptic comprehensible name of the DC. The Information class name field isn't filled in for all DCs since certain clients didn't understand its significance, so various DCs just have an English name.

Thus, while looking in DatCatInfo, picking English as the hunt language is ideal. • The Analyst remark, to be tended to during modification. Current Status, Future Work, and Difficulties This section has portrayed the relocation of language asset information classes from the unique Information Classification Vault to another Information Class Storehouse, by which the flawless information assortment is referred to mutually by the contraction DCR. Roughly a portion of the DCs from the Information Class Library have been moved to the new DCR, called DatCatInfo in the TermWeb climate (adding up to 2,977 DCs).

The leftover DCs have been kept in astatic archive.4 Be that as it may, much work stays to address the analyst remarks, orchestrate copies, rethink the chronicled DCs, and complete other cleanup errands. The essential test in this try will be organizing the work and tending to it in stages. Because of the endeavors of a group of workers, DatCatInfo has arisen as a new and worked on free open asset from a previous ISO project that might have in any case been dropped totally. Given the extent of work and backing that it requires, monetary help is desperately expected to accomplish its expressed objectives.

The overseeing board is looking for award potential open doors. A few difficulties are simply specialized. DC determinations contain a Steady Identifier (PID), for

instance: http://www.isocat.org/datcat/DC-1840. With the exchange to DatCatInfo, all PIDs are being changed appropriately; for instance, http://www.datcatinfo.net /datcat/DC-1840. Crafted by changing over the PIDs is still underway. Old ISOcat PIDs implanted in heritage assets will take steps to the new climate, in this manner keeping up with the necessity for perseverance innate in the framework. The administration strategies illustrated in ISO 12620:2009 don't matter to DatCatInfo. As noted over, another rendition of ISO 12620, portraying the administration of a DCR conventionally, has been supported by ISO/TC 37 for a 2019 distribution date. While DCs are no longer planned for formal normalization, strategies are as yet required for orchestrating copies, working on happy, belittling DCs, and tolerating new ones. New DCs will need to come from end-clients, so a commitment work process should be carried out. (Right now TermWeb has an element for submitting input, yet it won't get the job done.)

Characterizing these principal parts — administration methodology and public commitment work processes — is one of the most squeezing errands for the overseeing panel. The absence of consideration rules is a serious inadequacy. Such rules still up in the air. Key inquiries include:

1. What is a language asset? What kinds of language assets are served by the DCR?

2. What is an information class? What isn't an information classification?

3. How does an information class contrast from a semantic idea?

4. What are the phonetic spaces that the DCR ought to cover? Might they at any point be plainly characterized?

5. How might we obviously figure out what semantic space a DC applies to?

6. What rules ought to be utilized to decide if DCs currently accessible in a public asset ought to likewise be remembered for the DCR?

How might they be incorporated in order to keep away from overt repetitiveness and keep up with cash? The best test in creating and keeping up with DatCatInfo is the absence of subsidizing. For example, fostering the necessary commitment work process will require programming assets. Basically everything is as of now being completed by volunteers on a specially appointed premise. This part has navigated the historical backdrop of the DCR, following it from a simply paper standard, through its set of experiences as an Information Classification Library expected for organization by an ISO Enlistment Authority, to an Information Classification Storehouse unreservedly accessible on the web under an Imaginative Lodge permit. The advisory group answerable for the assortment will keep on tending to the harmonization and issues portrayed in this part be that as it may, as noted, there is no reasonable course of events for finishing this work.

What can be gained from this involvement with request to keep away from the variety in mission and harsh objectives that have denoted the advancement of the DCR? Surely, the absence of clear agreement on key perspectives, like consideration rules and topical spaces, can't be credited to any carelessness with respect to ISO/TC 37/SC 3, which set up and worked a DCR Administration Board for quite a long time and held endless gatherings and meetings in a work to characterize and accomplish shared objectives.

Broad conversation, arranging, cooperation, and generosity were put resources into the venture, and in any event, when confronted with troublesome occasions, for example, the deficiency of MPI as a significant benefactor, the work was friendly and without any trace of any misconceptions or clashes. Without a doubt, the dissimilar necessities and objectives mirror a worldview irregularity between the different networks of training that met up in great confidence. As Thomas Samuel Kuhn cautions, the sure dominance of basically a similar wording used to characterize the task in the end covered disparate necessities and practices. Maybe a more designated examination from the beginning could have uncovered issues of this nature prior, however once more, assuming that prominent rationalist of science is our aide, these sorts of indeterminacies are unavoidable.

6. Describing Research Data with CMDI- Challenges to Establish Contact with Linked Open Data

Introduction

The CLARIN (Normal Language Assets and Innovation Framework) research framework for the Sociologies and the Humanities (SSH) offers specialists access to an extensive variety of language-related research information and devices. The Virtual Language Observatory, for example, gives clients uniform admittance to almost 1,000,000 assets and apparatuses utilizing faceted pursuit on metadata, and by utilizing Combined Content Hunt clients can perform full-text look through across dispersed information bases. Furthermore, WebLicht upholds clients to handle language assets with predefined and client characterized device work processes, while the Language Asset Switchboard assists clients with interfacing assets with instruments that can deal with them.

The foundation relies upon a typical metadata structure that makes it conceivable to depict a wide range of assets to a fine-grained degree of detail, paying consideration regarding their particular qualities and the necessities of the numerous SSH people group. The Part MetaData Foundation (CMDI) follows a Lego block way to deal with metadata displaying, where rudimentary information descriptors are semantically grounded in idea libraries, and where parts can be characterized concerning those descriptors or predefined easier parts (ISO 24622-1:2015). This plan offers a typical syntactic premise, yet additionally boosts the semantic interoperability of CMDI-based metadata plans. Before, nonetheless, CMDI has not been utilized adequately to accomplish its full potential toward semantic interoperability. With the approach of the Semantic Web and the thought of Connected Information, obviously CMDI's interoperability guarantee is as of now restricted to the CLARIN universe and that information offering to different networks stays an issue that should be tended to.

In this part, we examine ventures toward broadening CMDI's semantic interoperability past the Sociologies and Humanities: We stress the requirement for an underlying information curation step, to a limited extent upheld by a connection vault that forces some design on CMDI jargon; we portray the utilization of power document data and other controlled jargon to help associating CMDI-based metadata to existing Connected Information; we show how huge pieces of CMDI-based metadata can be switched over completely to bibliographic metadata guidelines and subsequently went into library indexes; lastly we depict initial steps to convert CMDI-based metadata to RDF.

The underlying grassroots methodology of CMDI (implying that anyone can characterize metadata descriptors and parts) reflects the AAA trademark of the Semantic Web ("Anybody can express Anything about Any point"). Incidentally, this makes it hard to completely interface CMDI-based metadata to other Semantic Web datasets. This paper examines the difficulties of this undertaking. Inspiration CLARIN is an examination foundation that empowers Sociologies and Humanities researchers to get to and to handle language-related assets and instruments (Hinrichs and Krauwer 2014).

CLARIN offers four kinds of administrations:

(1) admittance to assets like reference corpora, lexical assets, and syntaxes;

(2) development of virtual assortments to join assets that help the investigation of examination questions;

(3) statement and filing of assets to oversee steady access and reference; and

(4) arrangement of electronic apparatuses that help researchers in the examination of literary information, for example, taggers, named element recognizers,

geolocation devices, and such.

Depicting the research is in this way fundamental material reliably and decisively to assist clients with finding the information, assess its handiness for the job that needs to be done, and access the information. The depiction system should be expressive to take special care of the huge assortment of information types, interoperable to help the sharing of depictions, adequately adaptable to expect future innovation changes, yet in addition sufficiently normalized to guarantee that the structure is embraced and utilized by the networks. Thus, CLARIN has chosen the

Part MetaData Framework (CMDI), which is a global norm (ISO 24622-1:2015). The initial segment of this section depicts CMDI, features its plan standards, and gives CMDI use models. The second part examines the difficulties to interface CMDI-based metadata to Connected Information.

A Circulated Framework The CLARIN framework is a circulated network across different foundations and nations, instead of a brought together center. This has both authentic and functional reasons. By and large, individual organizations have developed their own environments of storehouses for assets furthermore, instruments. The biological systems' plans frequently vary in nature at hierarchical and specialized levels with the goal that they can't be essentially joined into a solitary, focal, or general framework. Other than the distinctions in the specialized biological system of the establishments, assets at an establishment frequently have solid permit limitations forced on them so that such a asset (e.g., a paper corpus) can't be gotten to beyond the foundation, or access to the asset can be dependent upon severe confirmation and approval strategies. Moreover, organizations will generally have their own exploration specializations, and subsequently totally different sorts of examination information and apparatuses, alongside various approaches and specialized prerequisites to access and work with them. It is consequently better to keep up with all exploration dataunder the sponsorship of the establishment in control that made the asset, as opposed to endeavoring to concentrate the filing at a focal organization.

Additionally, circulated frameworks divide the gamble between the different partners and foundations, convey the assignment and cost for conservation, and hence work on the manageability of the framework. A Rich and Various Arrangement of Language Assets CLARIN offers a huge assortment of language assets, going from corpora with different (etymological) explanations, lexical assets, psycholinguistic investigations, advanced versions of books, communicated in language accounts and their explanations, jeopardized dialects documentation, and sentence structures to large information corpora that feed applications in the space of language advances.

The language assets come in a wide range of dialects, and keeping in mind that most assets are monolingual, many are bilingual or even multilingual, while others have many layers of comment to help their review. This assortment represents various difficulties that the exploration framework should adapt with. Given CLARIN's dispersed design, most specialized and authoritative issues are tended to at the partaking establishments. A bound together classifying, everything being equal, be that as it may, requires a focal way to deal with gather, comprehend, and fit their metadata portrayals.

The metadata portrayals need to have a degree of expressiveness that permits researchers to assess the importance of the assets they depict. Here, distinct classifications, for example, asset title, maker, size, or language as a rule don't do the trick to survey whether a given asset meets a researcher's requirements. Every one of the asset types benefits, truth be told from its own arrangement of elucidating implies. A lexical asset, for example, should be depicted with regards to the quantity of lexical watchwords/lexemes and definitions it contains, while such information classes are futile for, say, a text corpus. In the last option case, a researcher could really focus on a corpus' size (number of words), its language or dialects, its type-token proportion, its kind, etc.

Likewise, the translation of the metadata relies upon the unique situation. An asset with a size of five megabytes is somewhat little when the asset is multimodal material, yet rather enormous when it is a lexical asset. The arrangement of significant portrayals that assist specialists with either securely ignoring an asset or be provoked to explore the asset further is an issue of most extreme significance that any focal access to a dispersed framework should address. Depicting Language Assets Sufficiently In the library world, electronic assets are transcendently depicted with Dublin Center metadata (DC), a bunch of 15 enlightening classifications, like creator, title, distributer, year, and copyright holder (ISO 15836-1:2017). In the space of language assets, the Open Language Chronicle People group proposed its own metadata set.

It depends on the total arrangement of Dublin Center metadata terms,1 however the configuration permits the utilization of expansions to communicate communityspecific qualifiers (Simons and Bird 2008). One kind of language asset has its own encoding standard: Advanced releases of text are much of the time made accessible concerning the TextEncoding Initiative.2 The Text Encoding Drive (TEI) Rules for Electronic Text Encoding and Exchange incorporate a broad header that portrays the asset with metadata. More-expressive metadata designs are accessible in the library world, for example, MARC 21 (MARC-21 1999), and however this multitude of spellbinding compositions are both useful furthermore, successful in their unique situation, they need expressiveness to depict the fluctuating sorts of language-related assets.

There are three ways to deal with handling this issue: (1) build a rich arrangement of metadata descriptors to frame a solitary composition to portray all language-related research information; (2) build different patterns, each taking special care of a kind of language-related research information; and (3) build more modest parts to portray the different parts of language-related assets and afterward consolidate them in a secluded design to additional complicated patterns, one for each sort of language-related asset. CLARIN follows the third methodology.

Component MetaData Infrastructure (CMDI)

Different sorts of language assets require various arrangements of metadata (i.e., profiles). In CMDI, a metadata profile for a given asset type is worked by gathering pre-assembled parts, some of which are shared or reused across various blueprints, while others are well defined for the class of asset to be depicted. A CMDI part sections rudimentary information descriptors or other, less complex parts into a solitary unit.

We get, hence, a various leveled metadata framework (Broeder et al. 2011). Figure 6.1 shows a profile that can be utilized to portray text corpora. It has parts /GeneralInfo/,/Venture/,/Distributions/, and/Creation/, among others, that catch data that is free of the kind of the language-related asset. The resourcespecific part/TextCorpusContext/utilizes the two information descriptors/CorpusType / furthermore,/TemporalClassification/. Every descriptor should have a worth plan indicating the sort of its worth and furthermore should have a reference to its definition. In the given model, the ConceptLink has a handle reference, determinedly tending to the relating component in the CLARIN idea library (see beneath). Besides, it is determined whether an information descriptor is discretionary or required, or whether it might happen on different occasions. The two information descriptors show the expressive power expected to portray sufficiently an asset of type corpus.

The worth plan of/CorpusType/can take a worth from a predefined controlled jargon, which contains the expressions "practically identical corpus," "equal corpus," "general corpus," "reference corpus," "student corpus, etc. The controlled jargon for the component/TemporalClassification/contains the expressions "diachronic," "synchronic," "memorable," "present day," "other," and "obscure." Each rudimentary information descriptor, or information classification, ought to be characterized in an outer idea library, like the CLARIN idea vault (Schuurman, Windhouwer, Ohren, and Daniel 2016), or in its ancestor, the ISOcat library, which depends on the ISO 12620:2009 norm, or ought to allude to other laid out metadata plans, for example, the Dublin Center Metadata Set. Parts and profiles are characterized and put away midway in the Part Vault (Ďurčo and Windhouwer 2014a). The parts and profiles are characterized utilizing a Part Depiction Language; for each CMDI profile, the part vault can create a relating XML outline definition (XSD). Figure 6.2 shows the idea/corpus type/that is referred to from the profile for the portrayal of text corpora. This idea is characterized in the CLARIN idea library, the most frequently involved term library in the CLARIN people group. In the CLARIN Part Library, parts can be looked for, altered, or recently made. The part library has a public space that contains all parts that have been distributed, which get a uniform and constant ID so others can utilize them, too as a confidential space.

In the last option, new parts can be characterized, and explored different avenues regarding, before they might get distributed at a later stage. Figure 6.3 shows the XML portrayal of a CMDI occasion that depicts a text corpus. Note that the occasion alludes to its profile in the xsi:schemaLocation characteristic, and thus, standard XML innovation can be utilized to approve whether the example sticks to the construction. The CLARIN framework gives metadata modelers various instruments, for example, • The CLARIN part library (https://catalog.clarin.eu/ds/ComponentRegistry) also, the CLARIN idea vault (https://openskos.meertens.knaw.nl/ccr/program) for the definition and turn upward of profiles, parts, and information descriptors • COMEDI (http://clarino.uib.no/comedi), an online supervisor for CMDI metadata • SMC Program, an online device to imagine the progressive design of CMDI profiles; see https://clarin.oeaw.ac.at/smc-program/index.html

• CMDI2DC, a web administration that changes over CMDI-based profiles to Dublin Center (Zinn et al. 2016); see http://weblicht.sfs.uni-tuebingen.de/converter/Cmdi2DC/ The CLARIN focus vault at https://centres.clarin.eu/oai_pmh keeps a rundown of all CLARIN storehouses that give their metadata freely by utilizing the Open File Drive's Convention for Metadata Gathering (OAI-PMH). A focal center reaps all metadata at customary stretches and totals them into a solitary hunt list. The Virtual Language Observatory at http://vlo.clarin.eu/empowers clients to investigate the amassed datasets through twelve features and to play out a full-text search on the metadata. CMDI and Semantic Interoperability Previously, the CLARIN people group followed a grassroots way to deal with metadata the executives.

The CMD foundation, specifically the libraries, expressly upheld this development. Anyone locally was permitted and empowered to characterize metadata descriptors and parts, reflecting the Semantic Web AAA motto ("Anybody can say Anything about Any theme"). Thus, the libraries were quickly loaded up with descriptors to depict any conceivable part of a language asset. Frequently, clients didn't actually take a look at whether a sufficient descriptor or part previously existed. As opposed to utilizing a current one,new descriptors and parts were characterized higgledy piggledy. The impact of the grassroots development is reflected by the substance (many copies) and the size of the CLARIN vaults.

At the hour of composing, the CLARIN Idea Library gives more than 3,000 sections; the CLARIN Part Vault has in excess of 1,000 public parts and more than 180 public profiles. Obviously CMDI follows through on the grounds of syntactic interoperability. In view of XML, a CMDI example recording an asset is connected to a CMDI metadata composition, also, XML approval is utilized to check whether the example sticks to the diagram. The central concern to address is the understanding of the subsequent grammatical design. While most metadata components are grounded in the CLARIN idea vault, the translation needs to adapt to the enormous number of copy elements being utilized and their shifting logical installing. The CLARIN Virtual Language Observatory (VLO) tells the best way to manage this issue in a specially appointed way. To manage the enormous wide range of outlines, extensive portions of their information classifications are semantically planned to twelve VLO search attributes.3 Consider, for example, the feature "language," which files all assets as far as their language. In the CLARIN idea vault, there are something like four unique passages that characterize the information descriptor "language" here and there or other. There are additionally CMDI parts that allude to the Dublin Center component http://purl.org/dc/terms/language.

Every one of these sections are planned to the feature "language," considering that the information class is utilized in the "legitimate" setting. In the event that the information class is utilized in an "ill-advised" setting, say, to depict either the language of the asset's documentation or the local language of the asset's entertainer, the planning won't occur. While the planning helps fix the issue for the VLO, the multiplication of copied information descriptors should be tended to by the CMDI people group. Later on,

CLARIN jargon should be far superior made due. Clients ought to utilize existing, laid out terms at whatever point conceivable, as opposed to characterizing their own arrangement of terms. To ease the issue of relevant translation, when new terms should be made, definitions ought to be explicit as opposed to general.

To limit logical translation, for example, the descriptors /actorLanguage/and/documentationLanguage/ought to be liked to just/language/. The CLARIN people group has moved toward tending to the information curation issue. With the movement from the ISOcat vault to the SKOS-based idea library, the grassroots way to deal with idea definition has been changed to a more controlled climate where assigned individuals from the CLARIN people group ("public CCR facilitators") presently deal with the jargon. Likewise, a prescribed procedures manual for metadata displaying inside CMDI is at present being formulated. On the product side, the SMC program has been further created to follow the utilization of profiles, parts, and information descriptors across the CLARIN metadata set; it is a valuable device to help the curation of all current substance.

Besides, the CLARIN libraries are being gotten to the next level: The SKOS-based idea vault is simpler to use than the ISO 12620:2009-based ISOcat library, while the CLARINcomponent library presently adds a status to every part (one of Improvement, Creation, also, Expostulated). Information curation in the CMDI universe, in any case, stays a colossal test. Any change in a CMDI profile (a difference in a part or a rudimentary descriptor) should be reflected by a relating update in all

CMDI occurrences depending on the profile. With a million CMDI occasions beginning in 36+ CLARIN focuses, this is a difficult errand. By and by, information curation should happen, and it shows that Semantic Web innovation can uphold this cycle. CMDI and Connected Information The Semantic Web is worked from organized information of uniform asset identifiers (URIs) that are exceptionally interlinked. Berners-Lee (2006) characterizes Connected Information as tolerating these four standards:

1. Use URIs as names for things.

2. Use HTTP URIs so that individuals can look into those names.

3. At the point when somebody looks into a URI, give valuable data utilizing norms (Asset Portrayal System [RDF4], SPARQL Convention and RDF Inquiry Language [SPARQL5]).

4. Incorporate connections to other URIs, with the goal that they can find more things. With each CMDI profile and part in the CLARIN part vault, and each idea in the CLARIN idea vault being addressable with a persevering identifier, the CMD framework obviously satisfies the initial two circumstances.

The CLARIN people group requirements to deal with the excess two circumstances. For CMDI-based metadata to take part in Connected Information, it is important to add RDF backing to the CMD framework and to add connects to existing datasets. For the last option, we really want to plan both the CMDI metadata jargon to existing Connected Information (LD) jargon and the worth space of CMDI metadata to existing LD elements. In CMDI-based metadata, there are various chances to connect the worth space of information descriptors with Connected Information elements. Above all else, the names of asset makers, as well as the names of the foundations where the language asset started or on the other hand where it is facilitated, ought to be connected to URIs that allude to names. Authority Document Data Some CMDI metadata makers have begun to utilize authority document data (Trippel and Zinn 2016). A power document record gives the name of an individual or establishment a normalized portrayal. The power document record connects the normalized portrayal of a name with its elective structures or spellings to achieve

the objective of disambiguation.

Numerous libraries use authority records for character the executives. The Incorporated Power Record of the German Public Library (GND) has around 11 million sections, which incorporate over 7.5 million individual names and more than 1 million names for corporate bodies (DNB 2016). The Virtual Worldwide Power Document at viaf.org is a joint venture of more than 40 public libraries and is worked by the Web-based PC Library Center. The point of VIAF is to interface together the public power records of all undertaking individuals to a solitary virtual power document. Each VIAF record is related with a URI and totals the data of the first power records from the part states.

The Global Standard Name Identifier (ISO 27729:2012) at http://isni.org/holds almost 9 million characters, including over 2.5 million names of scientists and more than 500,000 association IDs. Later drives incorporate the Open Specialist and Giver ID (ORCID) at orcid.org and ResearcherID at researcherid.com. Every one of these power offices connect a uniform asset identifier to their records. Additionally note that numerous Wikipedia anecdotal articles allude to the URIs of the comparing authority organizations. Their datasets are likewise noticeable hubs in the Connected Open Information (LOD) project at http://linkeddata.org. The adaptability of CMDI permits us to handily characterize a CMDI part to hold authority record data.

Figure 6.4 shows the CMDI part/AuthoritativeIds/, which can be used to address at least one power records/AuthoritativeId/. Its most memorable component,/id/, stores the relentless identifier of the power organization, while/issuingAuthority/alludes to the organization that gives the information. All the previously mentioned organizations can be chosen as a worth of this descriptor. The creators have altered all CMDI profiles that depict research information from the College of Tübingen to incorporate this CMDI part for all information about people and associations. By and by, it shows that most of people alluded to in the CMDI metadata have a power record. If not, people can be approached to get an ORCID or ResearcherID. Likewise, most corporate bodies (like college establishments and other examination associations) can be connected to such records.

It shows that the GND from the German Public Library is a decent information source to connection to, making it conceivable to exceptionally recognize, say, either the College of Tübingen or its phonetics division as the maker of numerous conventional distributions (coming from library inventories), or to distinguish the examination information (coming from their vaults) it made. For additional subtleties, see Trippel and Zinn (2016). The creators trust that all CLARIN focuses follow this model and add authority records to their information. Utilization of Laid out Vocabularies Any common utilization of jargon upholds Connected Information. The CLARIN Part Library contains a few parts that utilize remotely characterized metadata terms.

The part/DcmiTerms/, for example, gives a CMDI-based portrayal of all DCMI Metadata Terms.6 To allude to dialects, metadata suppliers can utilize the CMDI part/iso-language-639-3/that addresses the three-letter language codes as characterized in the ISO 639-3:2007 code tables; see http://sil.org/iso639-3. 7 The CMDI part/Country/ makes accessible the nation codes as characterized by ISO 3166:2013. The last two parts are obsolete, in light of the fact that ISO has finished its help for URIs of the structure https://cdb.iso.org/cdb to allude to language and nation codes. While it is feasible to utilize the URI http://sil.org/iso639-3/documentation.asp?id=deu (or http://www.lexvo .organization/page/iso639-3/deu) to allude, say, to the ISO 639-3:2007 code for German (and to acquire more data about the referent), it is difficult to say whether the connections will remain resolvable a long time from now.

In this way, the CLARIN people group chose to import the ISO 639-3:2007 code set into CLAVAS, the recently made CLARIN jargon administration in view of OpenSKOS (http://openskos.org). This help means to give feasible, tenacious URIs to allude to ISO codes.8 Most CMDI information suppliers target utilizing a controlled jargon to recognize the media sort of an asset, however reference to such information utilizing the string datatype is frequently by the same token fragmented or incorrect, and in light of the fact that clients regularly avoid utilizing determined URIs. Express references to http://www.iana.org/tasks/media-types/media-types .xhtml are intriguing. Additionally, at the hour of composing, CMDI metadata suppliers utilize geological information bases, for example, geonames.org.

Other botched chances to allude to shared jargon remember the ISO 8601:2013 norm for dates and times, which is especially intriguing for the portrayal of sections and their term (spans) from accounts, records, comments, and so forth. Later on, the CLAVAS jargon administration might incorporate the IANA expressions and the other previously mentioned terms to address this issue.Link to Existing Vocabularies There is adequate potential to connect CMDI-based information classifications to the Semantic Web world, considering that all descriptors in the CLARIN idea vault are addressable by diligent identifiers.

To help information curation, semantic interoperability can be expanded by relating CMDI-based information descriptors to one another. For this, reevaluate the previously mentioned planning of CMDI information classes to features to help faceted perusing in the Virtual Language Observatory. Here, the planning is specially appointed as opposed to principled. In Windhouwer

(2012) and Ďurčo and Windhouwer (2013), the creators propose laying out unequivocal ontological connections between information descriptors. Utilizing another vault, the RELcat connection library, it becomes conceivable to lay out, for example, owl:same-as or skos:exaxtMatch relations between semantically comparable ideas, or to relate skos:closeMatch to nearly semantically comparable ideas. Later on, the CLARIN people group should utilize RELcat to formalize the VLO planning, and on the amazing scale it should force ontological understanding onto the 3,000+ sections in the CLARIN idea library.

Schema.org is a fascinating philosophy that CMDI metadata suppliers ought to consider utilizing. Take the class http://schema.org/PostalAddress, for example. It fills in as an anchor highlight address-related properties, the greater part of which have close to reciprocals in the CLARIN idea vault:/locationAddress/,/locationRegion/,/locationCountry/,/locationContinent/, /email/, and/faxNumber/. The term/address/could then be connected to PostalAddress, and the previously mentioned terms to its properties. In Zinn, Hoppermann, and Trippel (2012), the creators propose planning a portion of the sections of the CLARIN idea library to the schema.org metaphysics, to some degree to build CMDI's interoperability concerning the Semantic Web people group, and to a limited extent to help progressing curation endeavors inside the CMDI people group.

Up until this point, the CLARIN people group presently can't seem to examine and settle on a planning of CMDI jargon to schema.org or to vocabularies from other notable idea vaults or metadata plans. Here, the RELcat connection procedure ought to be utilized to formalize the planning portrayed in Zinn, Hoppermann, and Trippel (2012) and to enter other term equivalencies. Local area agreement could be set apart by connecting a status to each planning. From CMDI to Connected Information through Bibliographic Metadata Continuous work is expected to draw CMDI nearer to the library world and accordingly close to the Semantic Web. In Zinn et al. (2016), the creators propose crosswalks (along with an electronic converter) between CMDI-based profiles and the library metadata norms Dublin Center and MARC 21. Having a CMDI-based record switched over completely to MARC 21 assists its ingestion in the library with recording, however without power data the new data isn't connected to any earlier data in the list (e.g., normal creator or normal distributer), and subsequently is of restricted use.

With power document data, we can connect individual related metadata (specifically, the maker of an asset) with/dc:author/data in bibliographic data sets. This makes it conceivable to have a solitary section point for the customary distributions of a scientist and for the examination information the individual in question made. The same holds for foundations that assistance to make or host phonetic information and metadata.

The change of CMDI to Dublin Center accompanies a huge data misfortune; the change from CMDI to MARC 21 jelly a lot of data and is subsequently the favored bibliographic configuration. When a bibliographic organization has been achieved, there are existing converters to Semantic Web principles. From MARC 21, for example, there is a planning to RDF that can be utilized to create RDF triples.9 From CMDI to RDF by means of Direct Change In Ďurčo and Windhouwer (2014b), the creators propose a transformation from XML-based CMDI portrayals to RDF-based portrayals, tending to the third thing in BernersLee's (2006) list. The transformation incorporates all levels of the CMD information area: the CMD meta model as given in ISO 24622-1:2015, CMD profiles and part definitions, CMD idea definitions, and

RDF portrayals for CMD example information. Later on, the CLARIN part vault will offer RDF portrayals for all profiles and parts.

Here, the various leveled portrayal of a CMD part will be addressed by the part's URI (established in the CLARIN part library) and by a dab way to its subcomponents and components. At the hour of composing, the RDF transformation is continuous turn of events. A genuine transformation of CMDI-based RDF information requires information sharing at the URI level; that is, CMDI-based metadata should utilize URIs to allude to people, partnerships, geological spots, and other web substances. The utilization of power records in CMDIbased metadata portrayals fortifies the connections to other datasets, yet this must be the initial step.

With the semantic planning from CMDI jargon to existing Connected Information jargon still to be finished — the RELcat vault should be loaded up with some more passages — assessing the ampleness of the CMDI to RDF change algorithm is hard. Here, the local area should assemble more insight. RDF is the most widely used language of Connected Open Information. The information design accompanies RDF-based innovation for putting away or questioning datasets. Regarding metadata the board, nonetheless, RDF is less intelligible and harder to keep up with. Obviously, the CLARIN foundation best backings the record-based CMDI, so this is the compulsory arrangement today for all CLARIN information suppliers.

To receive the rewards of Connected Open Information, all reaped information ought to be changed over completely to RDF and made available through SPARQL endpoints. Given the disseminated nature of the CLARIN foundation, such transformation will be finished at the focal center point when all reaped information are accumulated and orchestrated. Here, the VLO is the best spot for gaining admittance to RDF portrayals of CMDI occurrences. Conversation The CLARIN people group has moved toward accomplishing semantic interoperability with different networks and toward connecting CMDI-based metadata with metadata accessible somewhere else.

The huge number of vocabularies accessible in the metadata world, be that as it may, appears to muddle the local area's work. Obviously, the CMDI people group should initially confront the test of arranging its own datasets. Given the conveyed idea of CLARIN, an extensive piece of this errand should be handled by the singular information suppliers. Every one of them benefits, nonetheless, from the CMD foundation, concerning the accompanying: a better CLARIN Idea Vault, where public CCR facilitators are currently in control to make due (and to organize) all terms; a CLARIN part vault that will need to offer (and to more readily promote) pre-assembled parts that are semantically grounded in the CCR and other term vaults; and a developing CLARIN RELcat connection library, where CCR terms can be ontologically connected both to one another and to outer vocabularies. With amazing asset support (the SMC program), information curation ought to be viewed in a serious way;

labor supply ought to be made accessible to address the curation and interoperability challenges sooner rather than later. The appearance of the Semantic Web and Connected Information offer inspiration too as applied and mechanical help for this errand. While information curation begins at home, it should not be restricted to CLARIN's own terrace. There exists a plenty of vocabularies in the metadata universe, and it is in many cases hazy which ones are ideal to utilize and how to utilize them successfully. Which of the vocabularies will continue through time, or if nothing else through various many years? While ISO principles are great applicants, the writers have as of now encountered that URIs to them become unresolvable, which thusly gives a persuading contention to set up one's own phrasing administration (like CLAVAS). In Cole, Han, Climates, and Joyner (2013), the creators likewise notice the test of "as well numerous semantic choices accessible for making RDF portrayals" in the library setting: early adopters of library LOD frequently have "fostered their own namespaces and semantics while distributing their index records as LOD informational collections." thus, the creators proceed, "there are an excessive number of sets utilized for library LOD informational indexes.

No single semantic net appears adequate for portraying library bibliographic information records." With the CMDI people group drawing nearer to the Connected Information world, we might arrive at a comparable resolution as to metadata records on language-related assets and instruments. Here, the CLARIN individuals ought to consider the prescribed procedures that are as of now being intended for changing bibliographic metadata into Connected Information (see, for example, Southwick 2015). In such manner, it merits underlining that the library world is likewise changing to the Semantic Web and Connected Information. The Library of Congress has

proposed another norm for library asset depiction called BIBFRAME, https://www.loc.gov/bibframe/.

While the Library recognizes the presence of various vocabularies (schema.org, Asset Depiction and Access [RDA], http://www.rda-rsc.org)

, the BIBFRAME jargon accompanies its own namespace.10 The creators of the bibliographic system by the Library of Congress (2012) recognize that "the proposal of a particular namespace is counter to a few current Connected Information bibliographic endeavors." Notwithstanding, they proceed, "it is urgent to explain liability and authority behind the schematic structure of BIBFRAME to limit disarray and diminish the intricacy of the subsequent information designs. It will be the job of the Library's norms partners to keep up with the associations between BIBFRAME model components and source vocabularies, for example, Dublin Center, FOAF,

SKOS, and future, related vocabularies that might be created to help unique parts of the Library work process."

The CLARIN people group might well choose to follow the illustration of a solitary namespace and to utilize the RELcat connection vault to connect, whenever the situation allows, to significant vocabularies that assume a significant part in noticeable Connected Informational indexes. End Previously, research information were not really open. They dwelled on recording reel-to-reel tapes, floppy plates, or hard drives, and to get to information it was many times important to contact the specialist who gathered the information in any case to learn insights regarding the information (for nothing) or to make a duplicate of the mentioned material.

A few foundations followed a methodical way to deal with gathering and documenting research information, and furthermore concocted their own metadata arrangement to help portraying and getting to the information. With various documents concocting their restrictive metadata language, it was hard, in the event that certainly feasible, for analysts to look across assortments. The CMDI structure for metadata targets cultivating syntactic and semantic interoperability. It empowers document maintainers and different clients to first characterize their enlightening jargon in idea libraries (or, whenever the situation allows, to utilize the jargon characterized there).

With the essential jargon set up, bigger metadata pieces, or "parts," can be characterized and made accessible to others in the CLARIN part vault. This grassroots development assisted chronicles with supplanting their exclusive depiction system with CMDI-based portrayals. These exploration information are routinely reaped from the a wide range of information suppliers at a focal spot. Following a curation and planning stage, the information are placed into the Virtual Language Observatory, which thus permits clients to play out a faceted-based search to enormous conglomerations of language-related material of a huge assortment. At this point, CMDI-based metadata have turned into the standard structure to depict language-related assets in the CLARIN people group. The CMDI people group actually should address various issues. In the first place, the CLARIN idea and part vaults need better curation.

In the two libraries, unused sections ought to be taken out. To manage copies and close to copies, information descriptors ought to be interlinked with one another to state their ontological connections. Additionally, their associations with terms from other metadata plans ought to be made unequivocal. Here, the RELcat connection library, which was first presented in Windhouwer (2012), ought to be at long last delivered and successfully utilized for this reason. Second, where relevant, jargon from laid out metadata plans, such as Dublin Center, ought to be utilized to depict viewpoints about an asset that are free from its sort.

With the utilization of laid out jargon as opposed to CMDI local terms, there is no requirement for a planning. Third, for upsides of descriptors, authority records from the library world ought to be utilized whenever the situation allows, as should ISO-based shut vocabularies for nations, dialects, dates, etc. Here, the CLAVAS jargon administration ought to be utilized whenever the situation allows, additionally to guarantee the diligence of all URIs. Fourth, it is beneficial that RDF become a vital piece of the CLARIN foundation. Both the part and the idea libraries ought to offer RDF trades and SPARQL endpoints for their entrances. Likewise, the VLO asset watcher ought to make accessible RDF-based portrayals of

7. Communicating Language Asset Metadata as Connected Information The Instance of the Open Language Documents People group

The Open Language Files People group (OLAC) is a worldwide organization of establishments and people who are making an overall virtual library of language resources.1 The library is virtual in light of the fact that OLAC doesn't hold any of the actual assets, maybe it totals an association list of the relative multitude of assets held by the taking part foundations. A significant accomplishment of the local area has been to foster norms for communicating and trading the metadata records that portray the possessions of a chronicle. Since its establishing in 2000, the OLAC virtual library has developed to incorporate north of 300,000 language assets housed in 60 taking part archives. Since every one of the taking an interest chronicles depict their assets utilizing a typical configuration and shared vocabularies, OLAC is capable to advance revelation of these assets through faceted hunt across the assortments of each of the 60 archives.3 The OLAC metadata standard endorses an exchange design that utilizes a communityspecific XML markup pattern. Meanwhile, Connected Information has arisen as a typical information portrayal that permits data from dissimilar networks to be connected into an interoperating all inclusive Snare of Information. This section investigates the use of Connected Information to the issue of portraying language assets with regards to OLAC. The first segment sets the pattern by portraying the OLAC metadata standard. The following segment examines Connected Information and how the current OLAC guidelines and foundation measure facing the guidelines of Connected Information. The third segment then portrays how we have carried out the transformation of OLAC metadata records into assets inside the Connected Information structure. At last, the fourth segment thinks about the effect on the OLAC framework, counting the two changes that have previously been executed to bring the assets of OLAC's taking part chronicles into the Phonetic Connected Open Information (LLOD) cloud (Chiarcos et al. 2013), as well as the capability of embracing Connected Information as the reason for a modified OLAC metadata standard.OLAC has made a foundation for the disclosure and sharing of language assets (Simons and Bird 2003, 2008d). The framework is based on three essential principles:

OLAC Interaction (Simons and Bird 2006), which characterizes the administration and guidelines process; OLAC Metadata (Simons and Bird 2008a), which characterizes the XML design utilized for the trading of metadata records; and OLAC Stores (Simons and Bird 2008b), which characterizes the necessities for carrying out a metadata vault that can be gathered by an aggregator involving the Open Chronicles Drive Convention for Metadata Collecting (OAI-PMH).4 The OLAC metadata conspire (Bird and Simons 2004) depends on Dublin Center, which is a standard initially evolved inside the library local area to address the recording of web assets. At its center, Dublin Center has 15 essential components for portraying an asset: Supporter, Inclusion, Maker, Date, Depiction, Arrangement, Identifier, Language, Distributer, Connection, Privileges, Source, Subject, Title, and Type. To help more noteworthy accuracy in asset portrayals, this fundamental set has been formed into an advanced arrangement of metadata terms (DCMI 2012) that can be utilized to additionally qualify these components. The capabilities are of two sorts — refinements that give more unambiguous implications to the actual components and encoding plans (counting controlled vocabularies) that accommodate normalized approaches to addressing the upsides of the components. The OLAC metadata design is characterized by a local area explicit XML diagram that adheres to the distributed rules for addressing qualified Dublin Center in XML (Powell and Johnston 2003). As well as supporting the encoding plans characterized by the Dublin Center Metadata Drive, those rules give a component to further expansion through the joining of use explicit encoding plans. The OLAC local area has utilized its principles cycle to characterize five metadata expansions (Bird and Simons 2003, Simons and Bird 2008c) that utilization controlled vocabularies intended for language assets: • Subject Language, for relating to accuracy (utilizing a code from the ISO 639 standard)5,6 which language an asset is about • Semantic Sort, for grouping the design of an asset as essential message, vocabulary, or language portrayal • Semantic Field, for indicating a pertinent subfield of etymology •

Talk Type, for demonstrating the etymological kind of the material. • Job, for recording the parts played by unambiguous people and foundations in making an asset Coming up next is an example metadata record in the XML design recommended by the OLAC Metadata standard as it has been distributed by the Lyon-Albuquerque Phonological Frameworks Information base, or LAPSyD. The depicted asset gives data on the phono-sensible stock, syllable designs, and prosodic examples of the Cape Verde Creole language. The model beneath shows the total metadata record as it is returned in a GetRecord solicitation of the OAI-PMH: /oai:record> In the model, we can see the fundamental elements of OLAC metadata. Metadata components come from the 15 components of the essential dc namespace, in addition to the extra refinements from the dcterms namespace. The xsi:type property is utilized to announce the encoding plot that is utilized to unequivocally communicate a worth. At the point when the encoded esteem comes from a controlled jargon that is identified in one of the OLAC proposals recorded over, the olac:code characteristic is utilized to encode the worth. All things considered, the component content can alternatively be utilized to explicitly communicate the signification more.

For example, the last component in the model above represents utilizing an ISO 639-3 code to distinguish the language and adding a note to say all the more explicitly that the asset relates to a specific lingo. Enter Connected Information At the point when OLAC started, creating reason explicit XML markup for data exchange was a best current practice. In the mediating years, Connected Information (Berners-Lee 2006; Bizer, Heath, and Berners-

Lee 2009) has risen up out of the Semantic Web7 movement of the Internet Consortium as a system for connecting dissimilar reason explicit datasets into a solitary interoperating worldwide Trap of Information. The catalyst for reexamining OLAC metadata as far as Connected Information has come from two headings. The first is the general direction of the Dublin Center Metadata Drive and the more extensive library local area. Custodians are perceiving that Connected Information addresses a chance for libraries to coordinate their data assets with the more extensive web (see, for example, Byrne and Goddard 2010). While Dublin Center was at first imagined as a straightforward record design, a new best practice has arisen in which a theoretical model8 is utilized in characterizing application profiles9 that furnish semantic interoperability with different applications inside the Connected Information system (Bread cook 2012). There is maybe no more grounded proof for a significant pattern toward Connected Information in recording than the BIBFRAME10 drive at the Library of Congress, which is expanding on the Connected Information model to foster a trade for theMARC standard (Mill operator et al. 2012).

Players in the OAI-PMH world are likewise working with Connected Information (Haslhofer and Schandl 2008, 2010; Davison et al. 2013). The subsequent catalyst has come from the utilization of the Connected Information structure to the connecting of phonetic information and metadata (Chiarcos, Nordhoff, and Hellmann 2012). With the rise of a Semantic Connected Open Information cloud (Chiarcos et al. 2013), OLAC as a significant wellspring of semantic metadata has been remarkable by its nonappearance. The work depicted thus has subsequently tried to correct this hole by carrying OLAC into the cloud of Connected Information. What does it take to interface into the Trap of Information? The Connected Information worldview depends on four straightforward standards (Berners-Lee 2006): 1. Utilize uniform asset identifiers (URIs) to name (recognize) things. 2. Use HTTP URIs so that individuals can look into those names. 3. At the point when somebody looks into a URI, furnish them with valuable data utilizing RDF and other Semantic Web principles. Incorporate connections to other URIs with the goal that clients can find more things. These principles act as the background for the conversation in the following areas, which portray how OLAC assets have been communicated as Connected Information and how those articulations have been integrated into the OLAC framework. As the principles demonstrate, the Connected Information worldview is based on two primary guidelines. The first is the Asset Depiction Structure (RDF),11 which is a model for the portrayal and trade of information that is semantically interoperable. The second is Uniform Asset Identifiers (URI),12 which give a language structure to the making of universally exceptional names for things on the planet (counting ideas).

The RDF way to deal with semantic portrayal can be summed up as follows. Data is communicated as a bunch of explanations. Every assertion is a triple comprising of a subject, a predicate, and an item. The subject is an asset that is named by a URI. The predicate is a URI that names a property. On account of addressing Dublin Center in RDF, the metadata components (like Title, Date, Maker) become properties. The item might be one more asset named by a URI or it could be a strict worth. A bunch of explanations frames a coordinated chart, in which the assets what's more, literals are hubs and the properties are guided circular segments from subject to protest. The reality that any assortment of RDF diagrams can be converged into a solitary, huge chart shapes the premise for the interoperation across information sources inside the Connected Information approach. Communicating OLAC Metadata as Connected Information OLAC is a hotspot for data around three sorts of assets: the controlled vocabularies it has created for language asset depiction, portrayals of the files that partake in OLAC, and portrayals of the language assets those documents hold. The following three subsections depict how each of these is communicated as Connected Information. A last subsection thinks about the issue of individual and hierarchical names, which is a region where the ongoing arrangement isn't yet in accordance with the standards of Connected Information. Controlled Vocabularies The OLAC Metadata Utilization Guidelines13 determine many accepted procedures as far as controlled vocabularies that ought to be utilized in addressing the upsides of the metadata components. To agree with the principles of Connected Information, those values should be addressed as URIs. Every one of the controlled vocabularies that are determined as encoding plans in Dublin Center (like DCMI Type and Emulate Type) as of now have URIs and RDF depictions in normal use.

This incorporates the ISO 639-1 and ISO 639-2 norms for language recognizable proof, which are carried out at the Connected Information Service14 of the Library of Congress. For case, the 639-2 code [deu] for German is addressed by http://id.loc.gov/jargon /iso639-2/deu.

Work is underway to carry out the whole ISO 639-3 code set in something very similar way at the LC Connected Information Administration; meanwhile, we are utilizing lexvo.org URIs — for model, http://lexvo.org/id/iso639-3/deu. The four controlled vocabularies characterized by OLAC itself (Phonetic Sort, Etymological Field, Talk Type, and Job) were not recently executed in RDF. These have presently been executed as hash namespaces, so that "vocabulary" from the Etymological Kind jargon is presently addressed by http://www.language-archives.org/jargon/type #vocabulary. The vocabularies are executed in RDF through the Basic Information Association Framework (SKOS).15 The jargon in general is first characterized as an example of an idea conspire. For example, coming up next is the meaning of the Etymological Kind conspire. This RDF test (similar to every one of the examples that follow) is communicated in the N316 language structure. The primary line is a finished subject-predicate-object triple in which "a" is shorthand for the property rdf:type. A semicolon shows that the following line will be another predicateobject pair for a similar subject, though a comma demonstrates an extra item for the same subject and predicate:

OLAC distributes a file of all taking an interest archives18 that connects to a portrayal of each document. By righteousness of expanding on the OAI-PMH, each chronicle has been relegated a novel identifier all along, and these are planned to HTTP URIs to give an area to the document depiction. For example, the HTTP URI for the LAPSyD document that is the wellspring of the example OLAC metadata record given above is http://www.language-documents

.organization/chronicle/www.lapsyd.ddl.ish-lyon.cnrs.fr. Along these lines, regarding file depictions, OLAC previously agreed with the initial two guidelines of Connected Information. Be that as it may, similar to the third rule is concerned, a RDF type of the depiction was absent. The OLAC chronicle portrayal is a required part of an OLAC metadata repository.19 It was at that point relegated a namespace and was characterized by a XML schema.20 Giving a RDF delivering of the document depictions included first making a RDF schema21 that characterizes the properties of an OLAC chronicle portrayal and afterward carrying out a XSLT script that changes the document depiction as gathered from the storehouse into the RDF same. For instance, coming up next is the RDF depiction of the LAPSyD document

Note that in the first dc:publisher proclamation, the LAPSyD chronicle (as depicted in the RDF piece in the former subsection) is pronounced to be the distributer of the metadata record. This is a utilization of the fourth rule of Connected Information wherein the objects of the RDF explanations ought to connection to other URIs so clients can find more things. The utilization of OLAC-explicit vocabularies is seen start with the olac:author property, which comes from the OLAC Job jargon. In the following two explanations, the property estimations come from the OLAC Field and OLAC Type vocabularies, individually. A last component of note is in the last articulation that depicts the subject language of the asset. In the OLAC metadata standard, first the subject language is distinguished by a code from ISO 639-3 as the worth of the olac:code property and afterward free text might be included the component content to give more significant subtlety.

This is converted into two RDF proclamations, one with a HTTP URI as the worth and the other with an exacting string as the worth. In creating the last option, which is a remark for human utilization, the change cycle prepends "Note for [kea]:" to recognize which ISO 639-3 language the remark is about. The Issue of Individual Names Having carried out the changes portrayed above, OLAC is presently communicating language asset metadata as Connected Information. There is one regard, nonetheless, in which the outcomes still miss the mark regarding the soul of Connected Information in that they neglect to consent to the fourth rule of Connected Information: "Incorporate connections to other URIs with the goal that clients can find more things." The trouble spot is the utilization of strict strings to address the names of people who are supporters of the language asset. In the particular instance of the asset depiction above, the client ought to have the option to follow a URI to figure out who "Maddieson, Ian" is. For the act of Connected Information across an overall crowd, the URI of an individual's article in the English Wikipedia is a famous wellspring of URIs for people. Stunningly better for Connected Information designs is the comparing URI from DBpedia, which maps each Wikipedia article into a RDF asset. Inside the library recording world, the best quality level is to utilize an identifier from a public library's position record — as, for example, the Library of Congress Name Authority File. In this specific case, Ian Maddieson is an adequately prominent language specialist that he can really be viewed as in both, however that won't be the situation for by far most of individuals who add to language assets. A current single source of URIs for north of 34,000 people across the field of etymology is the Language specialist Rundown Index of Linguists,24 however these URIs are not great for use in Connected Information since they are not "Cool URIs."25 Another source that gives much more URIs, however that needs consistency, is private or expert landing page URIs. The scholastic world has perceived the need to foster a normalized approach to remarkably distinguishing the people who have made commitments to the scholastic writing.

In 2012 an open, not-for-profit, local area based exertion named ORCID (Open Scientist and Patron ID)26 was sent off. In only four years, its library has developed to incorporate over 2.5 million special analyst identifiers. All coming up next are hence HTTP URIs that could be utilized to recognize this specific creator in a Connected Information setting (however note that just dbpedia.org, id.loc.gov, and orcid .organization conform to each of the four standards of Connected Information). At present the OLAC Metadata Use Guidelines27 suggest just that a benefactor be recognized "through a name in a structure that is prepared for arranging inside a sequential list." Yet the OLAC foundation has no method for upholding this rule or even of guaranteeing that every benefactor metadata component names just a single giver. As a result, regardless of giving a faceted hunt service28 that offers interoperable inquiry on 14 features that have uniform metadata values across the local area of chronicles, giver isn't one of those aspects. This is a region where the local area should fix its metadata rules and practices assuming that it plans to help the recognizable proof of supporters both in Connected Information and in faceted pursuit.

Integrating Connected Information into the OLAC Foundation OLAC has made the main strides of integrating Connected Information into its framework. The

new RDF vocabularies portrayed before are set up, just like the RDF changes for file portrayals and language asset depictions. The URIs for this multitude of assets are arranged following W3C best practices to help HTTP content negotiation29 so that they return a HTML record of course, yet return a RDF/XML archive when the header of the HTTP demand explicitly requests the application/rdf+xml Emulate type. To contribute30 to the haze of Semantic Connected Open Information (Chiarcos et al. 2013), the daily metadata reap makes a gzipped dump31 of the RDF/XML delivering of each metadata record in the OLAC list, and that dataset has been enlisted at the DataHub32 of the Open Information Foundation.Looking to the future, the OLAC metadata standard has not changed obviously since adaptation 1.0 was embraced in 2003. Considering the pattern toward Connected Information in the more extensive metadata local area, this present time might be a fitting opportunity to foster a form 2.0 update that brings OLAC into line with Connected Information as well as other current accepted procedures. Doing so would urge the partaking chronicles to make metadata that better interoperates with the worldwide Snare of Information. The open-enddedness of the Connected Information approach would additionally permit files to make considerably more extravagant metadata by enlarging their asset portrayals with properties from any RDF jargon.

Maybe the best benefit would be the longterm benefit for the supportability of the OLAC vision that could build from going into the standard of library rehearses. In any case, there is a drawback: Creating OLAC 2.0 would have a significant expense as far as requiring taking part documents to reimplement their OLAC vaults. One way forward is take on a cross breed approach. The OLAC gatherer could uphold both OLAC 1.1 and 2.0. All 2.0 metadata would be back converted into 1.1 organization so that all current administrations keep on working. All the while, all 1.1 metadata would be forward converted into 2.0 organization and took care of into a RDF aggregator that could catch all the added wealth of 2.0 metadata. OLAC could then start to foster new administrations that make the most of the Connected Information worldview, including offering semantic hunt over the OLAC inventory by giving an endpoint to SPARQL (the inquiry language for RDF).33 End Given the guiding principle of the OLAC interaction, one of which is that choices be made by agreement and that the best voice is given to the individuals who are carrying out the guidelines, refreshing the OLAC metadata standard to another rendition in light of Connected Information is not a stage that can be messed with. Moving to OLAC 2.0 would be a significant exertion requiring the taking an interest documents all over the planet both to concur and to reimplement. In any case, the time is most likely ready for OLAC to think about such an update to its principles and framework, especially considering the potential for a future wherein its language asset depictions could interoperate flawlessly with the more extensive library classifying local area — and even all the more comprehensively with the worldwide Trap of Information

8. TalkBank Assets for Psycholinguistic Investigation and Clinical Practice

The development of an organization of Etymological Connected Open Information (LLOD) can contribute in a large number significant approaches to the progression of the investigation of language structure, use, handling, what's more, securing. The sections in this book present a far reaching outline of different endeavors to assemble this new construction. The ongoing section will show how the TalkBank framework has previously prevailed with regards to acknowledging a significant number of these objectives and could ultimately uphold still others. TalkBank had its beginnings in 1985 with the Youngster Language Information Trade Framework (CHILDES), established by Brian MacWhinney and Catherine Snow; both the first and second creator of this part keep on attempting to develop and keep up with its developing assets.

TalkBank (https://talkbank.org) is presently the biggest open store of information on spoken language. At first, these information were addressed fundamentally in record structure. Notwithstanding, new TalkBank corpora presently incorporate linkages of records to media (sound and video) on the expression level, as well as broad explanations for morphology, sentence structure, phonology, signal, and different highlights of communicated in language. A significant rule hidden the TalkBank approach is that every one of its information are deciphered in a solitary reliable configuration. This is the Visit design (talkbank.org/manuals /chat.pdf), which is viable with the Faction programs (talkbank.org/manuals/family .pdf). This configuration has been created throughout the years to oblige the requirements of a wide scope of examination networks and disciplinary viewpoints. Utilizing transformation programs accessible inside Faction, the Visit configuration can be consequently changed over both to and from the arrangements expected for Praat (praat.org), Phon (phonbank.talkbank.org), Energy (tla.mpi.nl/apparatuses/energy), CoNLL (universaldependencies.org/format.html), Blacksmith's iron (blacksmith's iron -software.org), EXMARaLDA (exmaralda.org), LIPP (ihsys.com), SALT (saltsoftware .com), LENA (lenafoundation.org), Interpreter (trans.sourceforge.net), and ANNIS (corpus-tools.org/ANNIS).

For every one of these changes, the Talk design perceives a superset of data types (dates, speaker jobs, intonational designs, follow markings, etc). This intends that, when information are changed over into different arrangements, there should continuously be a technique for safeguarding information types not perceived in those programsagainst misfortune. This is finished in two ways. To start with, clients can frequently conceal Visit information in exceptional remark handles that are not handled by the program but rather that will be accessible for trade. Second, while utilizing different projects, clients should be mindful so as not to change codes in Visit design that mark perspectives that can't be perceived by different projects.

There are no cases where data made in different projects can't be addressed in Talk, since Talk is a superset of the data addressed in these different projects. TalkBank is made out of a progression of specific language banks, all utilizing a similar record organization and principles. These incorporate CHILDES (https://childes.talkbank.org) for youngster language obtaining, AphasiaBank (https://aphasia.talkbank.org) for aphasia, PhonBank (https://phonbank.talkbank.org) for the investigation of phonological turn of events, TBIBank (https://tbi.talkbank.org) for language in horrible cerebrum injury, DementiaBank (https://dementia.talkbank.org) for language in dementia, FluencyBank (https://fluency.talkbank.org) for the investigation of familiarity improvement/jumble, HomeBank (https://homebank.talkbank.org) for daylong accounts in the home, CABank (https://ca.talkbank.org) for Discussion Examination, SLABank (https://slabank.talkbank.org) for second language procurement, ClassBank (https://class.talkbank.org) for investigations of language in the homeroom, BilingBank (https:// biling.talkbank.org_ for the investigation of bilingualism and code-exchanging, LangBank for the review and learning of old style dialects, SamtaleBank (https://samtalebank.talkbank.org) for Danish discussions, the SCOTUS corpus in CABank with 50 years of oral contentions connected to records at the High Court of the US, and the expressed piece of the English Public Corpus, likewise in CABank.

We and our teammates are persistently adding corpora to every one of these assortments. The ongoing size of the text data set is 1.4TB and there are an extra 5TB of media information. Every one of the information in TalkBank are unreservedly open to downloading also, examination, except for the information in AphasiaBank, HomeBank, and research information in FluencyBank, which are secret phrase safeguarded. The Group program and the related morphosyntactic taggers are free and publicly released through GitHub (http://github.com). These data sets and projects have been utilized generally in the exploration writing. CHILDES, the most established and generally broadly perceived of these data sets, has been utilized in north of 6,500 distributed articles. PhonBank has been utilizedin 480 articles and AphasiaBank has been utilized in 212 distributions. As a rule, the more drawn out a data set has been accessible to scientists, the more that its utilization has become coordinated into the essential examination system and distribution history of the field. Metadata for the records and media in these different TalkBank data sets have been gone into the two significant frameworks for getting to semantic information: OLAC (see Simons and Bird in this volume) and CMDI/TLA (see Trippel and Zinn, additionally in this volume). Each record and media document has been doled out a PID (long-lasting ID) utilizing the Handle Framework (www.handle.net).

What's more, every corpus has gotten a DOI (computerized object identifier) code. The metadata accessible through these frameworks, alongside the information in the individual documents, executes every one of the prerequisites of the DTA instrument framework

(Blume et al., this volume). The PID numbers are encoded in the header lines of every record document and the DOI numbers are placed into HTML site pages that incorporate broad documenta-tion for every corpus, photographs and contact data for the givers, and articles to be refered to while utilizing the information. This large number of assets are intermittently synchronized utilizing a set of projects that depend on the way that there is a totally isomorphic various leveled structure for the Talk information, the XML renditions of the Visit information, the HTML pages, and furthermore the media records.

In the event that data is absent for any thing inside this equal arrangement of structures, the refreshing system reports the mistake and it is fixed. This data is then distributed utilizing an OAI-PMH (www.openarchives.org/pmh) viable technique for gathering through frameworks like the Virtual Language Observatory at https://vlo .clarin.eu (VLO) created through the CLARIN drive (https://clarin.eu). For 10 of the dialects in the data set, we give programmed morphosyntactic examination utilizing the MOR, POST, and MEGRASP programs incorporated into Group. These dialects are Cantonese, Chinese, Dutch, English, French, German, Hebrew, Japanese, Italian, and Spanish. Labeling is finished by MOR, disambiguation by POST, and reliance investigation by MEGRASP. Insights about the activity of the taggers, disambiguators, and reliance analyzers for these dialects can be found in MacWhinney (2008). Handling in every one of these dialects includes varying computational difficulties.

The intricacy and semantic detail expected for examination of Hebrew structures is maybe the most broad. In German, exceptional strategies are utilized for accomplishing tight examination of the components of the thing state. In French, stamping different examples of suppletion in the verb is significant. Japanese requires very various codes for grammatical features and reliance relations. In the end, the codes delivered by these projects will be fit with the GOLD philosophy (Langendoen in this volume). What's more, we register a reliance punctuation investigation for every one of these 10 dialects, which we will blend with the All inclusive Reliance tagset (https://universaldependencies.org). Since these morphosyntactic analyzers all utilization an equal innovation and result design, Family orders can be applied to every one of these 10 dialects for uniform calculation of records like MLU (mean length of expression), vocd (jargon variety), stop length, and different proportions of disfluency. Also, we have mechanized languagespecific measures like DSS or Formative Sentence Score (for English and Japanese) and IPSyn.

Following the strategy for Lubetich and Sagae (2014), we are presently creating language-general estimates in light of classifier examination that can be applied to each of the 10 dialects involving the codes in the morphological and syntactic reliance examinations. Nonetheless, there are numerous different dialects in the data set for which we don't yet have morphosyntactic taggers. This implies that it is fundamentally important to build MOR frameworks for dialects with a lot of CHILDES and TalkBank information, like Catalan, Dutch, Indonesian, Clean, Portuguese, and Thai. Utilizing these information and strategies, analysts have had the option to assess the utilization of various ways to deal with practically identical information. Such examinations have been especially productive in investigations of the securing of morphology and sentence structure. For instance, the discussion between connectionist models of learning and double course models zeroed in on information in regards to the learning of the English past tense (Marcus et al. 1992; Pinker and Ruler 1988; MacWhinney and Leinbach 1991) and later on information from German plural development (Clahsen and Rothweiler 1992).

In sentence structure, emergentists (Pine and Lieven 1997) have utilized CHILDES information to expound an itembased hypothesis of learning of the determiner class, though generativists (Valian, Solt, and Stewart 2009) have involved similar information to contend for inborn classes. Also, CHILDES information on the side of the Discretionary Infinitive Speculation (Wexler 1998) have been dissected in differentiating ways utilizing the MOSAIC framework (Freudenthal, Pine, and Gobet 2010) to show limitation based inductive learning. In these discussions, and numerous others, the accessibility of a common open data set has been urgent in the improvement of examination and hypothesis. Through these different strategies for record design transformation, metadata distribution, linguistic investigation, and information sharing, TalkBank has proactively satisfied a large number of the objectives of the LLOD project. Because of these endeavors, TalkBank has been perceived as a Middle in the CLARIN organization (clarin.eu) and has gotten the Center Trust Seal (https:// coretrustseal.org). TalkBank information have likewise been remembered for the SketchEngine corpus device (http://sketchengine.co.uk). Notwithstanding, there are different objectives of the LLOD project that appear to be as of now out of the reach of communicated in language corpora like TalkBank.

The sort of linkage proposed by Chiarcos and partners (this volume) and maybe even the LAPPS framework (Ide, this volume) would require a significant work to cross-file the individual lexical or morphological things in the numerous TalkBank data sets. Such linkage seems OK for lexical data sets or coding frameworks, in light of the fact that these include linkages that can straightforwardly yield optional examinations. For model, linkages between WordNet frameworks (http://wordnet.princeton.edu) in different dialects or linguistic coding highlights (Langendoen, this volume) can straightforwardly work with a assortment of NLP (normal language handling) undertakings, like interpretation, labeling, allegory examination, and data extraction. Be that as it may, the worth of linkages between substances for communicated in language corpora presently can't seem to be illustrated. For these corpora, the job of individual lexical things relies altogether upon the generally speaking syntactic and talk setting, and it isn't clear the way in which these relations can be assessed through basic connections on the lexical or featural level. For these assets, the main insightful devices include corpus-based look, for example, those accessible in the TalkBankDB framework at https://talkbank.org/DB. An unexpected issue confronting the assignment of linkages across communicated in language information emerges from the way that numerous server farms don't make their information freely accessible.

For instance, most of the materials in The Language Chronicle (tla.mpi.nl) can't be straightforwardly gotten to, and many are not accessible for access by any means. The materials gathered by the Etymological Information Consortium (ldc.org) are simply accessible to supporters, in this way making them beyond reach for connected open access. Of the significant information bases for communicated in language information, as it were TalkBank gives totally open admittance to records in a steady XML design. Subsequently, TalkBank would appear to be a decent objective for mix into the LLOD project, once techniques for managing communicated in language corpora have been created. As opposed to zeroing in on LLOD linkages across communicated in language corpora, TalkBank has created different strategies for between-corpus linkage. Two of these techniques have as of now been talked about. The primary technique includes the development of projects that can change over between Visit organization and configurations utilized by other insightful projects. That work has to a great extent been finished. The subsequent technique is the development and distribution of metadata to the VLO framework for ordering corpora, records, and media. This work, as well, has for the most part been finished. We are presently effectively participated in the improvement of a third way to deal with between-corpus linkage.

This strategy licenses programmed quantitative correlations between corpora or subsections of a given corpus. The objective here is to have the option to think about information from speakers at various ages, communicating in various dialects, in various assignments and circumstances, at various phases of learning, and with various clinical profiles. Yet to be determined of this part, we will frame the improvement of one of these strategies, called KIDEVAL, for contrasting youngster language information. An equal framework, called EVAL, has likewise been produced for making examinations across tests of discourse from people with aphasia (PWAs).

The EVAL framework utilizes the way that the information in AphasiaBank were completely gathered with a solitary reliable convention. In light of these convention information, we can extricate bunch implies for individual aphasia types (Broca's, Wernicke's, anomia, worldwide, transcortical engine, and transcortical tactile), which we can then use as correlations for the outcomes from individual PWAs. For kid language information, we have distinguished a subset of the data set that can be utilized in a comparable method for making correlations inside age gatherings. Examinations of this kind are major to the course of clinical evaluation, as well concerning the investigation of fundamental formative cycles.

Kid Language Test Examination For the evaluation of kid language capacities, language test investigation (LSA) gives a extremely serious level of natural legitimacy and "validness," as commanded by current instructive strategies (Overton and Wren 2014). It supplements normalized evaluation by giving a preview, so to speak, of a given youngster's language "in real life." All the more fundamentally, it gives pattern bits of knowledge into the kid's assets and shortcomings across the scope of language abilities important for age-proper correspondence, from jargon to linguistic structure to pragmatics. These abilities can be followed in normal settings over the long run

(Value, Hendricks, furthermore, Cook 2010). LSA gives clinicians substantial objectives for treatment far-fetched to rise out of consequences of state administered testing however that can be focused on for intercession (Overton and Wren 2014). Without standard referred to evaluations for youngsters talking non-standard tongues or English as a Subsequent Language, LSA likewise can give not so much one-sided but rather more educational data about a youngster's expressive language abilities and requirements (Caesar and Kohler 2007; Gorman 2010). Nonetheless, there are various down to earth issues in involving LSA for clinical purposes that will generally decrease the recurrence (and profundity) of its utilization in genuine clinical practice (Gorman 2010).

While oneself revealed utilization of LSA has been consistently moving in reports from 1993 to 2000 (Hux 1993; Eisenberg, Fersko, and Lundgren 2001; Kemp and Klee 1997), most SLPs (Discourse Language Pathologists) report ordering moderately short examples progressively documentation and utilizing them basically to register mean length of expression (MLU; Value, Hendricks, and Cook 2010; Finestack and Satterlund 2018), regardless of the way that MLU is definitely not a decent independent measure for distinguishing language weakness (Eisenberg, Fersko, and Lundgren 2001). Likewise, Lee and Jog (1971) saw that as short of what 33% of respondents registered an extra measure, the most famous being DSS. As of late, Finestack and Satterlund (2018) viewed that as just around 30% of American SLPs figure "casual" language test measures. Of these, from 86 to 94% (contingent on period of youngster) utilized MLU. Type-token proportion (TTR) was utilized by around 25-32% of respondents. Utilization of DSS had tumbled to generally 15% of SLPs, and different measures were utilized by less than 10% of SLPs who directed LSA. It is very much recognized that great LSA can be very tedious (Overton and Wren 2014). A few investigations have assessed that it requires as long as 8 hours of preparing and from 45 minutes to one hour of work after a record has been produced to process DSS (Long and Channell 2001; Cochran and Masterson 1995). One review (Gorman 2010) assessed that it requires over 30 minutes for every example following record to figure the Record of Useful Sentence structure

(IPSYN; Scarborough 1990). Hand calculation of most LSA measures, even the revered MLU, is very inclined to blunder.

It is challenging to utilize the same worksheet to process numerous phonetic measures, and it is an exercise in futility to move transcribed scrawls of what the kid said to most scoring conventions. Along these lines, even by selfreport, LSA isn't utilized by numerous clinicians, and isn't seriously taken advantage of by most to illuminate kid language evaluation. The people who do LSA frequently utilize an example that is far as well short to meet the planned example size for the actions that are processed (Westerveld and Claessen 2014), once in a while 50-75% less expressions than suggested. PC helped LSA can tackle every one of the issues recorded above (time, exactness and profundity of examination; Heilmann 2010; Value, Hendricks, and Cook 2010; Evans and Mill operator 1999; Mill operator 2001; Hassanali 2014), however isn't habitually utilized practically speaking. A new study assessed that just 12.5% of SLPs in Australia use PC helped record what's more, examination (Westerveld and Claessen 2014), and there is close to nothing to recommend that their American partners utilize such techniques at an essentially higher rate (Value, Hendricks, and Cook 2010). Finestack and Satterlund (2018) as of late found that PC helped LSA was utilized by just 1-5% of American SLPs.

As we will recommend, utilization of PCs to help with test record and examination, especially utilizing free utilities like Faction that also connect the example to a sound or video-recorded record of the kid's genuine discourse test, can significantly work on the speed, precision, and education of language test examination and, likewise, can likewise help with clinical appraisal, treatment arranging, and estimation of remedial advancement. In this section, we will show the utility of LSA led utilizing Faction and the KIDEVAL utility that utilizes two separate datasets. The first is an enormous companion of exceptionally youthful youngsters followed as a component of a solitary research The second is a survey of information acquired from the CHILDES Task Chronicle that we use to assess the likely utility of specific LSA measures at specific ages.

Numerous LSA estimates need powerful regulating or examination reference values, in this way the information in CHILDES can extraordinarily expand what we presently know through measures like MLU, DSS, IPSYN, VOCD, and others.In this part, we sum up how we have utilized the KIDEVAL utility to evaluate the dyadic connections of a huge companion of babies and their moms (n = 125), who were examined at 7, 10, 11, 18, and two years as a feature of a bigger report inspecting potential indicators of later youngster language abilities (Newman, Rowe, and Ratner 2015). The extent of the undertaking was very overwhelming: We had ~125 families and directed 5 play meetings, with both youngster's and mother's verbal communication being a focal point of investigation. This delivered a sum of approximately 1,250 quarter-to half-hour minute records. Given customary evaluations of time required per record to process numerous actions, we assessed an all out time responsibility of 6,250 hours to complete this piece of the undertaking, and the giving organization didn't, as a matter of fact, foresee that we would get any discoveries during the real award time window. Be that as it may, they were wrong.

This is on the grounds that Family media linkage in Walker Regulator, a Faction program utility for record of communicated in language, permits single keystroke playback of the section being interpreted. This chops down the time expected to make a precise record of the youngster's test by generally 75%. Additionally, on the grounds that the typographer can without much of a stretch over and over look at the record to the first, exactness is expanded. Then, we utilized the robotized MOR capability to dole out and disambiguate linguistic portrayals of the relative multitude of words in these 1,250 records. The order "mor *.cha" will run MOR, POST, and MEGRASP in grouping on all target record documents. The result has the type of this extract: Following the running of MOR and POST, we then, at that point, utilized the KIDEVAL order to produce calculation sheet result of every youngster's (and parent's) language highlights on more than two dozen factors. A portion of these factors, like respite length and MLU, are normal across dialects; others including explicit morphological highlights are remarkable and configurable to every language Shouldn't something be said about Standards? In checking on the writing on clinical utilization of language tests, LSA has all the earmarks of being utilized most frequently when state administered test information can't be gotten or are hard to decipher. It is by all accounts especially preferred for evaluation of exceptionally small kids.

Notwithstanding, there are reasonable issues in LSA for youngsters at two years old enough, which was the result estimation period for the babies in our review. A significant number of the regularizing or reference values depend on moderately couple of cases at least age ranges. For instance, for MLU, a somewhat ongoing report (Rispoli, Hadley, and Holt 2008) included 37 youngsters at 24 months. Mill operator and Chapman (1981), the exemplary reference for MLU in clinical practice, covered just 16 youngsters in this age section, while the biggest late review to report anticipated values for MLU (as well as number of various words, NDW) (Rice et al. 2010) had 17 commonly creating and 6 late-talking members in the age section from 2;6 to 2;11. These are not very enormous populaces on which to sum up impressions of a youngster's semantic profile, which is the reason a few specialists have communicated serious worries about utilizing MLU to distinguish whether a kid is normally creating or impeded (Eisenberg, Fersko, and Lundgren 2001).

For Type-Token Proportion (TTR) or NDW, the circumstance is comparative, since a large portion of the examinations referred to above likewise revealed these actions, and hardly any extra examinations are accessible. For DSS and IPSYN, reference partners are comparatively limited. DSS reference tables report on simply 10 kids from 24 to 27 months old enough (Lee 1974). In this age range, IPSyn gives information to 15 youngsters (Scarborough 1990). Our review doesn't plan to contribute regulating information on these actions right now. Nonetheless, we can show how the youngsters in our review performed on these actions (all were regularly creating, as is much of the time the case in research reports taken from moderately high SES families). By and large, information from this example show values for MLU, DSS, furthermore, IPSYN that are reliable with earlier, more modest examples (see figures 8.1-8.3). These information propose that KIDEVAL is a helpful clinical device for the evaluation of unconstrained language information in two year old youngsters, a gathering for which not many vigorous measures of LSA execution exist. Our outcomes are similar, and registered consequently, to information got from significantly more time-serious manual coding. In any case, we really do take note of that the unaffected example of Rice et al.

Accomplished higher MLU values than the other correlation associates. We likewise registered relationships among LSA esteems and state sanctioned test results at two years old enough. We got huge yet feeble connections that presumably legitimize bigger investigations of the accessible measures for babies and their build legitimacy. For occurrence, we associated the kids' MLU with IPSYN and DSS values; connections were critical. This ought not be astounding, since both IPSYN and DSS grant focuses for different syntactic components, and expressions with longer MLU values have more prominent chance to contain such highlights. In any case, it is maybe astounding that the real correlations are relatively low, even though they reach significance given our large sample size. (See figures 8.4–8.6.) In particular, DSS correlates more poorly with MLU than does IPSYN, in all likelihood because fewer utterances at 24 months meet DSS eligibility standards and because very early utterances do not achieve DSS sentence points. Likewise, IPSYN and DSS do not correlate well with one another, probably for the same reasons, indicating that they are not interchangeable assessments of a toddler's language sample.

Further developing Standards That's what our review recommends, at youthful ages in English, some potential LSA measures don't seem, by all accounts, to be estimating similar builds. Obviously, a solitary LSA measure (particularly MLU, which has been investigated broadly; Eisenberg, Fersko, and Lundgren 2001) can't give the entire picture, and doing various LSAs is far too tedious, except if more specialists and advisors use PC helped examination to produce information that are more receptive to these worries. We are, notwithstanding, energized by the way that the information from our enormous example of babies truly do look like those in more modest reference study reports. We likewise trust that psychometric assessment of certainty spans around mean qualities will be important to work on the vigor of measures like DSS and IPSYN for recognizing run of the mill and abnormal execution, despite the fact that we do have an information to illuminate this dynamic interaction. Fuller Help for SLPs We are current attempting to move the CHILDES Task Document from a vault and asset for scientists to a unique wellspring of reference information that can be utilized to evaluate furthermore, treat youngsters across the world's dialects. To this end, the TalkBank project is attempting to make the accompanying moves that ought to extraordinarily upgrade clinicians' capacities to apply LSA to a more extensive scope of youngsters all the more effectively and keenly: 1. Increment the quantity of dialects that can be naturally parsed and detailed utilizing Group utilities. As different supporters of this volume note, the free Group utilities now have syntaxes for an enormous number of dialects; this number is developing yearly.

In this way, clinicians working in Spanish, French, German, Dutch, Mandarin, Cantonese and other habitually utilized dialects currently have assets to perform exact LSA of dialects other than English. 2. Convey existing corpora in the CHILDES Chronicle to move along "standards" for usually utilized LSA result measures. We are presently during the time spent getting done with this second aggressive job. As of late, we finished KIDEVAL examination of an enormous arrangement of corpora (n = 630 youngsters), every one of whom spoke North American English, and every one of whom were participated in free play with their guardians (a comparable setting). Results have been genuinely intriguing, and we give just a brief taste of our discoveries here. To begin with, we are glad to take note of that Roger Brown's (1973) perception that MLU is most valuable when the kid is genuinely youthful or up until the point that it arrives at a worth of generally 4.0 gives off an impression of being approved by this enormous example, where MLU levels for our youngsters past these qualities and ages (see figure 8.7). We likewise note that IPSYN and DSS give off an impression of being differentially delicate to changes in progress in years, as do two elective approaches to registering lexical (jargon) variety — Type-Token

Proportion (TTR) and vocd (Malvern et al. 2004), a PC calculation less delicate to varieties in example size. Family reports both in the KIDEVAL utility (see figures 8.8 and 8.9). Like our discoveries revealed before for the Newman et al. concentrate on youngsters, IPSYN and Figure 8.7 MLU values for 630 youngsters in the CHILDES Chronicle. From N. Bernstein Ratner and B. MacWhinney, "Your PC to the Salvage ... ," Workshops in Discourse and Language 37, no. 2 (2016): 74-84, www.thieme

.com (reproduced by authorization). 144 Nan Bernstein Ratner and Brian MacWhinney DSS seem to quantify various things, especially across the more extensive age range covered by the CHILDES information. For instance, IPSYN shows up more delicate to development across very youth, though DSS gives off an impression of being more touchy at more established ages, maybe as a capability of the "sentence point" that gives more credit when a sentence is thought of syntactic, a significant build in recognizing common from abnormal turn of events as youngsters mature. TTR and vocd (see figures 8.10 and 8.11) show a to some degree more troublesome profile to assess. Vocd seems to follow better with age across this example than does TTR. Mutt rently, vocd is reported in a number of research reports (Pilar 2004; Silverman and Bernstein Ratner 2002; Owen and Leonard 2002; Wong 2010) but has no published norms; we hope to rectify this shortly. TTR has long been known to be vulnerable to a number of issues, particularly sample size; whether Vocd can improve on this to inform clinical assessment remains to be seen. Extending norms and evaluating the utility of various LSA measures is an ongoing initiative of great potential value to SLPs. We also note that there are no robust norms for LSA conducted with bilingual or English Language Learning (ELL) children, a major clinical cohort where LSA is used, given the parallel lack of standardized assessment norms for this population (Caesar and Kohler 2007). rently, vocd is accounted for in various exploration reports (Pilar 2004; Silverman and Bernstein Ratner 2002; Owen and Leonard 2002; Wong 2010) however has no distributed standards; we desire to in no time correct this. TTR has for quite some time been known to be defenseless against various issues, especially test size; whether Vocd can enhance this to illuminate clinical appraisal is not yet clear. Expanding standards and assessing the utility of different LSA measures is a continuous drive of incredible expected worth to SLPs. We additionally note that there are no hearty standards for LSA directed with bilingual or English Language Learning (ELL) youngsters, a significant clinical companion where LSA is utilized, given the equal absence of normalized evaluation standards for this populace (Caesar and Kohler 2007).

LSA is a significant instrument that one can use to evaluate and grasp kid language capacity in a naturally substantial manner. Having said this, it is underutilized for various reasons, basically in light of the fact that when done "the hard way," it is very tedious. Since it is tedious, we realize that clinicians don't completely take advantage of what can be realized from LSA, deciphering extremely short examples, and basically determining a couple of measures for example, MLU, which are not maximally useful for evaluation, treatment arranging, or result estimation. Media-connected record, for example, is accessible utilizing the free. Faction utilities accessible through TalkBank/CHILDES, incredibly speeds record of a kid's language test. When finished, this record can be utilized to produce quite a large number valuable, precisely registered proportions of kid language execution. These can be utilized both to increase other evaluation measures and to focus on focuses for intercession. Occasional LSA can likewise pass judgment on the youngster's advancement in language development, utilizing the first LSA as a benchmark measure. As clinically engaged programming advances, the youngster's record can be matched with different utilities, like PHON for phonological investigation, or FluCalc for familiarity examination, with minimal extra exertion. Group linguistic parsers can likewise empower clinicians to assess bilingual kids communicating in different dialects, a novel advantage while working with a developing and testing segment in our calling. When inquired as to whether they would utilize PC helped projects to break down language tests all the more rapidly and all the more usefully, most of clinicians in a new review concurred that they would, in the event that they could recognize how to achieve this (Westerveld and Claessen 2014).

We were fascinated to peruse of a fruitful experimental run program to utilize SLP partners or helpers to create records and measures utilizing SALT (Mill operator 2011), another LSA programming program. Hence, we are hopeful that volumes like this, alongside web instructional exercises and the proceeded with development of projects accessible to SLPs, will help clinicians to take advantage of the capability of LSA all the more completely. In total, the CHILDES/TalkBank utilities are an significant apparatus in a SLP's collection of clinical assets — free, efficient, and computationally strong.

So power up your PC and take PC helped LSA for a turn — for we anticipate that you will end up being a quick and steadfast fan. More extensive Ramifications We have analyzed top to bottom the manners by which the development and approval of the KIDEVAL program depend on correlation of a given kid language test with the bigger CHILDES data set. A comparative methodology inside the EVAL program empowers us to look at a record from a given individual who has aphasia with the more full AphasiaBank information base of 408 PWAs and 254 ordinary controls. Right now, we have just applied these strategies for English and French, yet they ought to function admirably for every one of the 10 dialects for which we can consequently figure morphosyntactic examinations. We intend to expand on our capacity to consequently register a wide assortment of measures such as MLU, IPSyn, DSS, TTR, and 12 others, by creating standard referred to clinical profiles like KIDEVAL (for youngsters) and EVAL (for grown-ups with language hindrance).

In spite of the fact that an action, for example, MLU includes a solitary build, measures like DSS, IPSyn, and QPA (Rochon et al. 2000) include a mind boggling blend of many choices about linguistic classifications and blunders. Utilizing projects to naturally process variation mixes of these fundamental choices, we will actually want to realize what bits of these bigger scoring frameworks are generally prescient of the real degree of language procurement during improvement, involving age as an intermediary for formative level. Work by Lubetich and Sagae (2014) has proactively shown that approaches in view of information mining techniques, for example, classifier development might have the option to beat these more seasoned standard measures. By acquiring programmed admittance to enormous corpora that can be consequently broke down, we will actually want to try out these very interesting opportunities for clinical determination and formative assessme.

9. Empowering New Joint effort and Exploration Abilities in Language Sciences The executives of Language Procurement Information and Metadata with the Information Record and Examination Device

The investigation of language is by definition interdisciplinary. It is arranged at the convergence of the humanities and the sociologies. To research the human limit with regards to language information, use, and obtaining, the field of etymology should incorporate logical strategies also, arrange itself among the methodologies of the different fields of mental science. Basically, key inquiries —, for example, knowing a language or how a individual gains a language — rely upon cross-phonetic examination, which can enlighten both the conceivable outcomes and the limitations on human language. Engaged by cyberinfrastructure, language concentrate on in quest for these inquiries can start to coordinate across disciplines and across dialects in another manner land can take part in the science unrest imagined ahead of schedule by the Public Science Establishment's Blue-Lace Warning Board on CyberInfrastructure (Atkins et al. 2003; see additionally Lave and Wenger 1991) and sought after in this manner (e.g., Berman and Brady 2005; NSF 2007; Borgman 2007, 2015; Abney 2011; G. Lord 2011; and T. H. Lord 2011). Our advanced and arranged age presently empowers phenomenal open doors for catching language securing information, consequently separating put away information for investigation and translation, and supporting vital cooperative grant.

It additionally presents new difficulties. In this section, we examine those open doors and we represent a way to deal with them through a contextual investigation — the development of a Virtual Semantic Lab (VLL)1 also, its cyberinfrastructure advancement of information catch and investigation devices. We first survey open doors and difficulties connected with information quality and information intricacy in the field of language acquisition.2. Then, we portray the framework of standards also, best practices that support the VLL. Then, at that point, we acquaint a cybertool focal with the VLL, the Information Record and Examination (DTA) tool,3 planned to empower information capacity, extraction, and investigation that lead to cross-semantic disclosures and cultivate cooperation. We will contend that the device, in view of precise metadata and information naming, as well as on adaptable phonetic comments, works with cooperative exploration across projects, research labs, dialects, and disciplines. We represent the utilization of the cybertool in cross-etymological hindrance, require an organized examination of information and formative perceptions. Albeit all phonetics tries searching for widespread etymological properties and the underpinnings of language require some level of cooperation, this is particularly significant for research on youngster language procurement, since recording, interpreting, and coding kid language information is both complex and tedious (Blume and Desire 2017). Albeit new advances offer extraordinary commitment in cooperative work, they likewise present challenges. It is notable that various scientists create and utilize various plans for recording and chronicling their information, frequently for authentic or logical reasons. Difficulties of documentation may likewise emerge inside a solitary task. Throughout a venture or a strand of examination, the scope of information that should be caught may develop, frequently in capricious ways that are affected by different advancements in the scientists' own work or in the field. Work in phonetics connected with this challenge has been in progress for quite a while.

For instance, E-Merge, the Electronic Metastructure for Jeopardized Dialects Data,7 is one current work to address the requirement for computerized information documenting principles informed by language specialists. The Overall Metaphysics for Etymological Depiction (GOLD;8 Farrar and Langendoen 2003; Simons et al. 2004; Cavar, Cavar, and Langendoen 2015; Langendoen, Fitzsimmons, also, Trickster 2005; Langendoen this volume) is a work to foster a metaphysics for phonetic portrayal on the web that can boost the handiness of connected semantic information made accessible to the more extensive local area (see Drinking spree and Langendoen 2010 for survey). The Open Language Documents People group (OLAC)9 tries to propel best practices in information chronicling and further to make an organization of information stores. The European Open Etymology Working Gathering (OWLG)10 develops Open Information sources in phonetics, including significant ontologies (OntoLingAnnot's ontologies, Pareja-Lora and Aguado de Cea 2010; Pareja-Lora 2012a, 2012b, 2013).

Notwithstanding, to all the more completely address the test of organizing linkage, we really want essential research instruments with the ability to adjust metadata, in this way permitting spread and access, and furthermore ready to venture profoundly into semantic investigations of language information to connect fields across dialects, datasets, and projects (see "The Information Record and Examination Device Engages Revelation in Trial Information" segment later in this chapter).11 In the event that a specific degree of normalization is accomplished, the language specialist can seek after the commitment of programmed explanation (as accomplished by CHILDES for morphosyntactic comment in as numerous as 10 dialects now, cf. Bernstein Ratner and MacWhinney, this volume), which would extraordinarily help the information creation process.

Cross-semantic exploration likewise requires catch of exact data about various levels of semantic portrayal (e.g., explicit discourse sounds in an expression, morphological markings, the manners in which words are gathered in expressions and sentences). Late innovation empowers the reconciliation of many degrees of information depiction and investigation, on the grounds that linkage among information focuses permits information to be placed and controlled effectively across levels.Addressing these difficulties in the field of language securing requires apparatuses with normalized designs for information catch, yet additionally with adaptability and space to develop.

Given that a focal objective in cross-phonetic investigations of language obtaining is to find the similitudes and contrasts in formative examples across dialects, it is especially significant not exclusively to normalize information yet in addition to acclimatize realities got from freely planned examinations, endeavoring to follow examples and make determinations from broadly fluctuating information gathered in broadly various ways (e.g., Phillips 1995 and Color et al. 2004).

The intricacy of language information stretches out past the attributes of semantic structures. It incorporates systemic and research plan data, data about information provenance (metadata), and media portrayal of information notwithstanding markup (i.e., coding) along numerous aspects (e.g., semantic properties of explicit words, morphology, expressions, and sentences) during investigations (for a conversation of related metadata issues, see Desire et al.

2010).14 Catching these many elements of information is time-and work serious. Making use of innovative chances to catch various components of information might prompt lumbering and, surprisingly, counterproductive apparatus in the event that the mechanical devices are not intended to boost productivity of information catch and examination that works with joint effort.

Utilizing a organized advanced climate not just empowers the catch and extraction of numerous levels of basic semantic data, yet in addition benefits analysts generally. To start with, metadata might be caught all the more methodallly. Instruments for information catch can provoke the analyst to remember data for significant metadata fields.

Upgrades of this type assist with normalizing metadata documentation across ventures and research centers and in this manner support likeness (Desire et al. 2010; Blume and Desire 2017). Second, information might be better saved and gotten to. On the off chance that information are not safeguarded along with metadata approving information provenance, they can't dependably support cooperative examination, replication, or reanalysis.

Protection, in any case, brings its own difficulties. As Bird and Simons (2003) and members in the GOLD task have noted, as innovation changes, information accumulated specifically organizations might gamble with misfortune, featuring the requirement for an economical furthermore, dependable cyberinfrastructure. At long last, great information catch frameworks can be utilized as instructive devices on the side of educating information the board abilities. Understudies in all fields of language procurement require broad preparation in phonetic examination of language information, yet in addition on the observational and trial techniques utilized first to gather language information and afterward to lay out the metadata fundamental for their safeguarding, scattering, and cooperative use. As called attention to by G.

Ruler: All the more critically, when we show we ought to make sense of that information sharing and replication is a vital part of the logical cycle. Understudies need to grasp that quite possibly of the greatest commitment they or on the other hand anybody is probably going to have the option to make is through information sharing. (G. Lord 2011, 270) In this section we will show

steps we have made toward making a cybertool that is planned to empower proficient catch and conservation of language information on the side of col- laborative cross-etymological language securing research, subsequently connecting more-worldwide metadata explanation to more-explicit phonetic information comment. Improvement of Electronic Cyberinfrastructure On the side of the Language Sciences:

The Virtual Semantic Lab (VLL) Contextual investigation and the DTA Instrument Advancement of cyberinfrastructure should include innovation improvement as well as likewise vested local area improvement (see Borgman 2015 and Blume and Desire 2017, part 14, for a conversation of these issues). The Virtual Etymological Lab (VLL) is the consequence of a project created by establishing individuals from an expanding Virtual Community for the Investigation of Language Acquisition,15 whose objective is the formation of a digital empowered worldwide and interdisciplinary virtual exploration and learning climate. It was created to empower scientists to share aligned research techniques during the essential examination process and likewise to practice and show logical strategies and best practices for information assortment and the executives in essential examination.

The VLL houses a progression of electronic courses coordinating coordinated and nonconcurrent types of intuitive data dissemination that show understudies explicit techniques for exploring language information. These courses are intended to be shown related to the VLL research strategies manual (Blume and Desire 2017). The DTA Instrument An electronic Information Record and Investigation (DTA) device is essential for the center of the VLL also, its courses. The DTA device gives an organized connection point to metadata and information assortment; it not just aides scientists and understudies in the essential exploration process, counting information the board, yet it likewise brings about an online aligned data set of constantly growing cross-phonetic information in addition to an Examination Bank.

The Investigation Bank records plan and strategic variables associated with every specific trial (or naturalistic review) through which language information are gathered. The DTA instrument follows the research standards and practices depicted in Blume and Desire (2017) and expects to be just the analyst knows about them. The instrument connects to a related arrangement of constantly extending information from in excess of 20 dialects gathered north of 30 years by the Cornell Language Procurement Lab, different labs, and individual analysts across the US and abroad.

The DTA device hence gives an information bank coming about because of the records and examinations it stores. Notwithstanding, it contrasts from different information banks, like CHILDES, in that it is basically planned as an essential examination instrument, organized to normalize metadata and information passage, the executives, and investigation; to allow the smoothed out correlation of information across datasets and projects; and to cultivate sound cooperative examination with shared information, as portrayed underneath (see the VLL and VCLA sites for the VLL assets and for the vision and mission fundamental the undertaking; additionally Desire et al. 2005, 2010; Blume, Flynn, and Desire 2012; Blume and Desire 2012b, 2017, particularly section 14).

The DTA device gives a web interface that directs the specialist bit by bit through the cycles of producing, putting away, investigating, and getting to information. It coordinates information into projects that contain fundamental data, for example, analyst names, reason and driving speculations, results and conversation of the venture, all to give an outline of what the project is about. The venture level additionally remembers data for project members (subjects), and references. Each undertaking has conformed to its foundations' IRB/Human Subjects standards for endorsement.

Licensed innovation privileges are safeguarded by creator (head examiners) arrangements. Human subjects' secrecy is safeguarded by permitting access to the full arrangement of subject data just to approved scientists (others can get to the information, however private data is covered up). Each venture has at least one datasets. The datasets are gatherings of information coordinated by any rules applicable to the review (e.g., subject age, language, explicit examination task utilized), and remember data for recording meetings, records, and coding. The DTA device guides clients in the catch of data at the meeting level in four essential regions: principal data, assets, records, and codings. The information fields on the meeting primary data screen incorporate metadata (e.g., term and area of a meeting) that assistance to lay out information provenance.

An assets screen gives linkage to unique, crude sound or crude video records, or to transcribed and examined records as well as field noticed that give information credibility. Figure 9.1 epitomizes the task, dataset, and meeting levels of DTA device coding. Other than organizing the way that clients contribute the two information and a wide cluster of metadata (Pareja-Lora, Blume, and Desire 2013), the DTA device permits one to connect fields across datasets and projects. Through a secret key security framework, individual clients can be given admittance to individual ventures or sets of activities. Project data (e.g., driving theories, philosophy, exploratory batteries, or point by point subject data), results, furthermore, conversation can be added.

The DTA device tracks distributions, related examinations, and book index connected with an exploration project. Subsequently, each undertaking incorporates a test bank in which every one of the information, metadata, and parts of a review are made sense of exhaustively. This degree of detail permits scientists and understudies to know precisely the way in which a specific report was led, and hence allowing replication is central.

Since replication is an undeniably significant worry in sociology research, knowing precisely the way that information were gathered and investigated is essential for information reanalysis and for the production of crosslinguistic near plans. Examination and Educating Notwithstanding the DTA device, course materials in the

VLL incorporate organized varying media materials for exhibit and practice; virtual studios; a specialized client's manual (Blume and Desire 2012a) to give preparing to understudies on the utilization of the DTA device and the Examination Bank; showing materials, for example, address slides; admittance to the exploration techniques manual (Blume and Desire 2017); a bunch of materials to aid information assortment, information the executives, and information examinations (e.g., a multilingualism survey for evaluation of

degree and nature of multilingualism,17 Blume and Desire 2017, 238, fn7); and stages for significant distance conversation and coordinated effort. These materials are incorporated into a cyberinfrastructure to oblige the high-accessibility requirements of distance learning programs (Blume, Flynn, and Desire 2012; Blume and Desire 2012b). In the information local area of the VLL, eight colleges in the US and one in Peru18 gave the establishment to VLL improvement and development, both broadly and globally, by adding to and partaking in a first series of interuniversity courses that have been directed based on its assets. Establishing individuals additionally contributed and shared both instructing and research models and materials, driving to a different arrangement of varying media tests accessible to specialists, instructors, and understudies the same.

A bunch of distributions creates exhaustively the instructive viewpoints (Blume and Desire 2012b; Blume et al. 2014), specialized viewpoints (Desire et al. 2005; Blume and Desire 2012a; Blume, Flynn, and Desire 2012; Pareja-Lora, Blume, and Desire 2013), and reasonable angles

(Desire et al. 2010) of both the VLL and the DTA device (Blume and Desire 2017, 264-267). In what follows we will embody the utilization of the DTA device in quest for dynamic exploration inquiries in the field of language obtaining.

Utilizing both test and normal discourse information, we will start up the improvement of DTA instrument explanations and question capabilities to address the difficulties of explicit and adaptable information markups that are fundamental for crosslinguistic investigations. Correlations of English-French and English-Spanish information will represent, with information gathered by the VLL people group. An Illustration of an Exploration Challenge: The Procurement of Relative Provisions One exploration region that has been stood up to by the VLL, with help from the DTA instrument, includes the procurement of relative provisions. The intricacies of this area require coordinating explicit information catch at the sentential level with the metadata addressed in the DTA device (e.g., figure 9.1).

* 9 7 8 9 3 5 6 6 7 9 3 6 8 *